MONEY MILESTONES

A twelve-month personal personal finance journey

DR. JESSE CARLUCCI

Paperback ISBN: 978-1-09835-802-0
ebook ISBN: 978-1-09835-803-7

Printed in the United States of America

MONEY MILESTONES

Foreword

Money Milestones: A twelve-month personal finance journey is an exploration of personal finance as it relates to different events, seasons, holidays, and cultural changes across the year. The 12 chapters each correspond to a month and discuss a relevant personal finance topic for that month. For example, "January" discusses new beginnings and finding the self-motivation to start making better financial decisions. July is the most common month that Americans take a vacation, and that chapter focuses on how to budget for and save money during vacation. When taken as a whole, the twelve-month journey tells a story of not only yearly milestones but also milestones throughout the readers' financial lifetime. So, this book touches on all the major personal finance topics one would expect (investing, budgets, taxes, careers), but it does so in a completely novel way. My goal was to move beyond the more formulaic format of personal finance books and take an approach that explores how our personal finances change throughout the year. This is also a book about people. Wrapped into each chapter is some of the details of my own personal finance journey because my hope is that it will make many of the concepts more relatable. There is a complete financial plan presented across the 12 months, but my goal was to make an interesting narrative that includes reference to scientific studies, stories about people, and my personal experience in the financial planning world. For example, in "October" (Financial Vampires), I explain why certain vehicles "suck" away your cash like financial vampires but then also present a simple plan for how you should approach buying a new car. I think this makes the process of learning a personal finance plan far more interesting than just boiling it down to the numbers. By tying the advice to specific milestones across the year, my hope is that the advice is more immediately relevant and memorable to you.

Money Milestones doesn't just discuss personal finance in a bubble, presenting the optimal mathematical method for planning as part of a series of quick tricks or rules. Rather, it focuses on stories of people and their successes and failures. Sometimes those people are those that I've worked with as a financial planner or professor, and other times they are me. I made many financial mistakes when I was first starting out, and hopefully you can learn from what I did wrong. Sometimes these stories are just about regular Americans. In chapter ten, I tell the story of Chris Robinson, whose family lost over $100,000 because they purchased Beanie Babies in the 1990s as a long-term investment. Exploring the "cost" of making poor personal finance decisions is one of the persistent themes present across all 12 months. Sometimes that cost is monetary, other times the cost is less tangible, like relationships, success, or happiness. There are times where you might think you are reading a self-help book, and that is by design. There is an important link between your personal attributes like motivation, determination, and attitude, and your ability to stick to a financial plan. The inspirational stories in *Money Milestones* demonstrate that any ordinary person can break the cycle and build a successful financial future. Personal finance can often be a dry topic, but when these discussions are tied to people, holidays, and regular cultural rituals that all Americans think about throughout the year, I believe they are more interesting!

Chapter 1

January: New Year's resolution:
Find your financial self-motivation

Something changes inside you when you decide to spend four to six years inside a research laboratory staring into a microscope day in and day out for what feels like an eternity. The outside world disappears, and it almost feels like you've transcended reality and now the "micro-world" inside that microscope is the only thing that feels real. Anybody that has spent a significant amount of time doing scientific research knows that staying sane during the process really comes down to one important thing: dealing with the boredom. Collecting data of any kind requires repetition, counting, recounting, record-keeping, and often doing the same thing thousands of times over. The process is boring. There's no way to sugarcoat it, and it doesn't matter what field of research you are in. Maybe you are looking at genetic mutations as a biologist, looking at minerals under a microscope as a geologist, or recording reaction products as a chemist. The collection of data is a slow and tedious process. The interesting part comes later when you synthesize the results and can communicate with the world this new thing you discovered about how the universe works. It can be exhilarating to discover something new to science and push the boundaries of human understanding by even the smallest amount. But the process of getting to that point often requires dedication and isolation far greater than is comfortable by folks that need normal social interactions with their peers. Something has to keep them motivated to stay isolated in that lab when most would rather have been having fun with their friends. You are probably wondering why I'm starting a book about personal finance with anecdotes about science. As I mentioned in the foreword, I was an academic scientist and professor before changing gears and moving towards investment and financial planning. It became clear to me in the early stages of putting my ideas to paper (or laptop in this case) that successful laboratory scientists have something extremely important in common with people that are successful in personal finance. They are *self-motivated*. Self-motivated people can focus and pursue goals without oversight or "pressure" from an outside source, like a boss, parent, or significant other. The first year of college is often where self-motivated students separate themselves from those that need an external source of pressure to pursue accomplishments. Without a parent applying pressure to wake up and go to school every morning, many 18-year-old college freshmen find it overwhelmingly difficult to get out of bed and trudge down to listen to a 9:00 am lecture.

In 1966, an American psychologist named Julian Rotter published a paper in the journal "Psychological Monographs" that laid the foundations for the concept of "locus of control."[1] Simply put, locus of control (LOC) is the degree to which people believe that they have control over the outcome of the events in their lives as opposed to outside circumstances beyond their control. LOC is theorized as internal if a person believes they are in full control of those outcomes (because of their own choices) or external if those outcomes are controlled by outside factors which the person can't influence (such as fate itself). Consider the following statements:

"I wanted to save this month, but things just kept coming up that I had to pay for. I'll never be able to save enough money to retire."

"I decided to use this month's savings to treat myself to a fancy dinner and night out on the town. I'll re-budget and make up for it next month."

Person one clearly thinks that the universe has already decided they will never have enough money to retire. They placed the blame for their spending on nebulous "things" that came up, but they never took responsibility for their own role in producing the outcome. In contrast, the person in statement two knows they overspent for the month and takes responsibility for their role in causing the outcome and develops a plan to adjust accordingly the following month. Consider again the following:

"Mrs. Johnson is a terrible teacher; I would have passed the exam if she just explained things better."

"I should have studied more for Mrs. Johnson's test."

Assuming, of course, that Mrs. Johnson's test was reasonably fair, person one is showing an external LOC in this instance, because in their mind, nothing they could have done would have given them a passing grade on the exam. Person two understands that even if the test were difficult, they would have passed if they studied more. During my tenure as a college professor, I often noted that the students that were best equipped to deal with the rigor of research seemed to be more on the internal part of the LOC spectrum. When I started working as a financial planner, I noticed again that those with a more internal LOC seemed to be the ones that could stick to a budget, meet their retirement goals, and ultimately control their personal finances.

There are three other personality traits that I also think are crucially important to achieving success in personal finance, and all are more common in people with an internal LOC: *high self-efficacy, grit,* and a *need for achievement.* People with a high need for achievement (nAchs) tend to seek challenges, set high standards for themselves, and exhibit a high degree of independence in their daily lives.[2] Most importantly, nAchs tend to associate their accomplishments with their own abilities and like to set goals for themselves. It will become very apparent as you progress through this book that setting goals is extraordinarily important for success in personal finance. The need for achievement also can influence workplace dynamics, an effect first noted by psychologist David McClelland in his 1961 book *The Achieving Society.* nAchs tend to require attention for their efforts because they require to be constantly challenged and therefore want recognition when they accomplish the goal they set before themselves. David McClelland also found that nAchs will tend to find small tasks or challenges that were easier to accomplish if a larger goal was insurmountable. This is a fantastic mental framework to have when trying to control your finances because Rome wasn't built in a day, and neither will financial freedom be reached in a day. It requires small steps and mini achievements along the way.

The current undisputed king of personal finance books, courses, and podcasts is Dave Ramsey. His first book *Financial Peace* and follow up *The Total Money Makeover* have been wildly successful, with *The Total Money Makeover* spending 200 weeks on the *NY Times* best sellers list. The case of Dave Ramsey's success is often a source of contention for professional financial planners because there are certain mathematical inefficiencies in his plan, which are hard to reconcile with good financial advice. For example, Mr. Ramsey strongly suggests that his readers pursue a "debt snowball," where they pay their lowest debts first regardless of interest rate and then put that money into the next highest debt when the first one is paid off and so on. Mathematically, this is inefficient when compared to a "debt avalanche," where the highest interest rate debts are always paid first. So why does the debt snowball method seem to resonate with so many people across America if it means you waste money? The answer is simple. It triggers the achievement-based outlook of so many people. Accomplishing small tasks in a shorter amount of time reinforces to people that they are doing a good job and making progress on something that seems too big to tackle all at once. As we noted earlier, this is a personality trait of nAchs, and something that is necessary to accomplish your financial goals. I'm reminded of my own personal battle with obesity as a teenager, and how small achievements were necessary to break free of the mindset that was keeping me unhealthy. I was always a bit of a heavy kid, but after a few sports injuries as a teenager, I quickly became obese as my addiction to soda increased and my ability to be active declined from injury. By the time I was 18, I was 250 lb at 5'10" in height. I had tried many times to lose weight, but I always gave up because I never saw any progress. But then one day when I was in college, the number on the scale was 10 lb less than I expected. This achievement gave me a jump start, and with each 10 lb lost, I celebrated another small victory. After a year of hard work, I was down to 160 lb, and I've maintained a healthy weight for the last 20 years. All I needed were those small achievements along the way, and my entire worldview changed. I've seen the same light bulb go off when people finally take control of their finances. No longer do they view success as an insurmountable task that can't be solved without a huge increase in income but as a series of small tasks and achievements that put them on the path to financial freedom. In "February," we'll discuss "trimming the fat" from your budget, and how these small victories add up to an exceptionally large change in your financial status.

Along similar lines is the concept of self-efficacy. Self-efficacy is one's innate ability to achieve goals and execute a course of action to reach those goals. When I was younger and overeating and drinking too much sugary soda, I was exhibiting low-efficacy behavior. I knew the proper course of action to solve the problem, but I was unable to take it. I feel very strongly that these personality traits, which are so advantageous to a successful financial future, are changeable. I've seen the change in myself as I've evolved as a person who is better able to set goals, plan a course of action, and achieve them. When I was younger, many of these things eluded me. Other behaviors that correlate to low self-efficacy are smoking, improper use of birth control/condoms, seatbelt use, and dental hygiene. Simply put, people with low self-efficacy give up sooner and tend to abandon a course of action at the first sign of resistance. This is unfortunately something I see quite often in my work as a financial planner. If I agree to a monthly budget with someone with low self-efficacy, they often want to abandon the budget forever if a minor unforeseen expense comes up (auto repairs for example). The proper course of action would be to go right back to the monthly budget after the car repairs are completed! It is hard work to change your mindset to believe very strongly in your ability to control your finances (high self-efficacy), but like any other personality trait, you need to slowly build your confidence to change with small victories.

Recently, I was chatting with some friends that work in higher education, and one of them noted that they've seen a profound change in the character of many young people over the past 20 years. He mentioned that the students today seem to have no willingness to "dig deep" and push through a hard situation to overcome it. He didn't know it at the time, but what he was describing is the concept of *grit*. According to the Merriam-Webster dictionary, grit is defined as " firmness of mind or spirit or unyielding courage in the face of hardship." While I can't answer the question "are kids these days going soft," I do think that grit is essential to achieving not only your financial goals but also your life goals. Pioneering psychologist Angela Duckworth summarized much of her research on grit in the 2016 book *Grit: The Power of Passion and Perseverance.*[3] Her conclusion (amongst other things) was that all other things being equal (IQ, socio-economic status etc.), grit can explain why one person might be much more successful than the other. In other words, the most successful people react differently when they fail. They show an "indomitable spirit" to lift themselves back up and try again. In some cases, over and over until they eventually succeed. The key truth here is that failure is more important than success when it comes to learning about ourselves. How you react to a financial failure, crushing debt, or the loss of your job and income will play a significant role in your ability to be financially successful over your lifetime.

Many self-help gurus swear that the "power of positive thinking" and constantly repeating positive phrases to yourself can change your life and give you the grit required to overcome your negative emotions (anxiety, fear, jealousy). The problem with this type of positive affirmation is that they operate at a very superficial level and don't inhibit the core negative beliefs that many people have about themselves. However, there is a good amount of evidence that positive "self-talk" (internal monologue) can help increase your performance in motivational or athletic endeavors. In 2011, a team of sport psychologists from the UK summarized the research from 47 self-talk studies and were able to show that there was a consistent positive motivational benefit to using the technique.[4] This came as no surprise to me based on my own anecdotal evidence, hiking with my wife in the Canadian Rockies. My wife is a consistently better hiker than me. She doesn't get winded as easily and can hike miles of steep inclines without any indication that she needs a break. Imagine my surprise when I asked her about her exceptional conditioning, and she just laughed. She *would* often get extremely tired and exhausted but admitted that she "talks" herself through the hardest parts of the hike. She reminds herself that this is not an impossible task and that she literally needs to take it one step at a time. I had assumed that it was just easier for her, when in reality, she just had incredible determination. Nowhere is it more important to have these internal discussions with yourself than when making financial decisions. Do you *need* that $800 new iPhone or can you get by for another year with an older model? How much do you save each week brewing your own coffee as opposed to buying it from your local Starbucks or café? By constantly having an internal conversation with yourself, you can reinforce your motivational beliefs and change yourself for the better.

The title of this chapter is a bit of a ploy on my part. January is, of course, considered the time of new beginnings and a fresh start to the New Year, with many people fostering a brand-new perspective that they think will change their life. Logically then, it follows that we should start our personal finance journey by talking about how you are going to become (and stay) motivated to take control of your finances for the rest of the year. But there are some problems with using New Year's resolutions as a "start to a new beginning." First, resolutions are often used by people as a gauge of what they *think* they should be doing rather than what the person wants to do. Are those resolutions based on your needs or on society's expectations? Yes, you should build a budget this year or save for vacation or lose 30 lb for that great vacation you are saving for. But when push comes to shove, are you willing to do the work? If you were, you probably would have done it before January 1st. Many studies have shown that most people fail at completing their New Year's resolutions, particularly as they age. Similarly, most extreme or fad diets are simply too difficult for people to maintain over the long term. Dieting doesn't work. Lifestyle change does work. So, before you commit to really gaining control of your financial future, recognize that it is a lifestyle change that you should be doing all year long. Real goals do not start on New Year's, they are with us every day.

You may have noticed in the preceding pages, I mentioned "financial success" quite a bit. Self-motivation is indeed critical to be financially successful, but what exactly does it mean to be "successful" in this context? There are obvious measurements we can make to explore this, such as net worth, retirement savings rate and balance, debt, credit score, and home equity. We will explore these things in later chapters, and they are important. But they aren't what I mean by financial success. The number in the bank account is important but only to a certain extent. A large study by psychologist Andrew Jebb and others in 2018 found that emotional well-being peaked at around a salary of $75,000/year and $95,000/year was ideal for "life evaluation," which considers long-term goals and comparisons to others.[5] That suggests money gets you part of the way, but it is not the whole story. If money can't strictly buy our happiness, what is the alternative? I define financial success as having enough money to comfortably live the life you want to live. That could mean almost anything depending on your background, career, lifestyle, and goals. So personal financial success is not a "one size fits all" endeavor. As we go along this journey together over the next 11 months, it is important that you really think hard about what success means to you. Does it mean retiring at 50 and traveling the world? Or does it mean working until you're 70 because you are incredibly passionate about your career? Or maybe it just means that you can live a simple life and leave a legacy to your children and grandchildren. We'll revisit this in "December," but it should always be at the forefront of your thoughts.

Chapter 2

February:
Budget your way to financial freedom

The relentless chill of the winter months often forces people to stay indoors for long periods of time. Warmer places in the United States, such as Southern California, Florida and Texas, usually allow for normal outdoor hobbies in the winter, while folks in colder regions rely on indoor hobbies to prevent cabin fever. In the previous chapter, I casually suggested the reader find their self-motivation to permanently gain control of their personal finances. So to build on that, I'd like to chat about why extremely expensive winter activities, like skiing, might be a major hindrance to your financial success. There are plenty of free or cheap activities to pursue as alternatives while seeking sanctuary from snow and freezing temperatures. In February, we're going to build a budget and it seems appropriate to start by discussing indoor activities that won't break your budget!

One of the common themes that you see in personal finance books is "budget-shaming" or "spend-shaming". That is, the author "shames" the reader by telling them they shouldn't be spending money on some expensive luxury item, like a sports car, fancy jewelry, or expensive hobby. In *Money Milestones*, I do spend some time praising the budget-minded consumer, but I hope my readers don't get the impression that I'm shaming them for purchasing nice things. My point throughout (e.g., see chapter ten on financial vampires) is that some people can afford nice things, and others shouldn't be paying for them at the cost of their long-term goals. So, you need to understand yourself and your long-term needs for your money. Can you afford to spend $10,000 per year on jet-skis and model trains and still stay on track to accomplish your (much more important) goals in life? If so then your budget is going to look different than somebody living paycheck to paycheck. If money is tight, and you are looking for a way to pass the time affordably, there are many indoor activities that are easily placed into a budget. Additionally, these low-budget options are ideal for those that want to save money during the long winters we have in much of the United States. It is easy to spend a lot of money on the default entertainment options for most people—movies, bars, restaurants, and travel. It is much harder to entertain yourself when you are trying to save money.

During the 2020 coronavirus self-isolation and social distancing period, many Americans were suddenly exposed to a harsh reality. Sitting at home all day is boring. Similarly, many can get "antsy" during the winter months because they crave outdoor activities that tend to be more expensive. After considerable thought, I settled on a list of indoor activities good for February. These activities are considerably more cost-effective than expensive hobbies like traveling, skiing, attending concerts and events, eating at expensive restaurants, and so forth. I also threw in a few activities (e.g., hiking) which are good for warmer weather but are also extremely cost-effective. Again, to clarify, I'm not saying you shouldn't have nice dinners or go on expensive trips, but I'd like to provide some alternatives:

- Cooking, baking, and recipe making
- Board games (especially European-style strategy games)
- Painting (canvas and paints can be expensive, but there are cheaper alternatives like watercolor)
- Podcasting (listening and making your own)
- Hiking (most states have local trails that are free)
- Geocaching
- Editing Wikipedia
- Making music using free software
- Computer programming
- Genealogy
- Restoring furniture
- Yoga and other "at-home" exercises
- Thrift store flipping and online sales
- Mentoring/tutoring
- Fostering animals and volunteering at shelters
- Participating in citizen science projects
- Reading/writing

The beauty of these simple activities is that they don't require a large initial outlay of cash. Many of these activities are nearly free because the resources and infrastructure (state parks, websites/software) are already established. Others (e.g., board games, painting, reading) do require money, but they provide a massive amount of entertainment hours for comparatively small amounts of money. I call this Entertainment Time Value (ETV):

ETV = (Total cost per year) / (Total hours of entertainment provided per year)

The items on my list above are low ETV hobbies. They provide an individual or a group of people an activity that occupies a large amount of time relative to its cost. For example, imagine you purchase a board game like The Settlers of Catan or Ticket to Ride from your local department store. Each game takes about 1.5 hours, four people can play, and the current price for both is around $44.99. If you play that game four times over the next year, the total hours of entertainment = 4 x 1.5 x 4 = 24 hours. The ETV = $44.99/24 hours = 1.87. What does that number mean? It means that every hour of entertainment costs you only $1.87 for the whole year, assuming you played four times. Now imagine a group of four people go to the movies at a nice theater. Let's even suppose they don't want to see IMAX or 3D show, just a regular showing. According to *USA Today*, the average cost of a movie ticket during 2018 was $9.11. The total cost for that outing is $9.11 x 4 = $36.44. Sounds fairly good until you remember that a movie only lasts around two hours. With a total of 4 people x 2 hours = 8 entertainment hours. So, the ETV = $36.44/8 hours = 4.55. Or a $4.55 cost for every hour of entertainment. In this case, it doesn't matter how often you go the movie theater, it is always going to have an ETV of around 4.55, but our board game is reusable and will have a decreasing ETV the more it is played. So, in our example, you spend about three times as much to entertain yourself going to the movie theater than by playing a board game. As you can imagine, spending an evening at a nice restaurant, swanky bar, or concert will have an even higher cost per hour.

I know what you are thinking. How dare this nerd put a price tag on fun? While it is my job to evaluate things like this, I want to preemptively defend myself by saying that I also like fun. I enjoy fancy cocktails and restaurants, and I'd rather watch a new release movie in IMAX than on Netflix ten months later. But once you are aware of ETV (cost-hours), it will subtly change how you approach your entertainment spending. I hope you picked up this book because you are at least somewhat interested in making a change to your financial situation. I'm confident that being smart about entertainment spending is one of the fastest and most straightforward ways to make personal finance improvements. But while we're on the subject, how do you decide how much of your budget should go to entertainment?

One of the simplest and most impactful ways to secure your family's finances is to build and follow a simple budget plan. On the surface, it sounds easy. Just follow the plan and everything will take care of itself, right? The reality is that life tends to get in the way of budgeting, and people begin to lose track of where their money goes each month. They lose track of how many coffee drinks they purchase each week, their monthly subscriptions, what other family members are doing, or even how much they pay for basic utilities. Sticking to a budget can be a game changer for some people, especially for those that make a good income but still can't seem to get ahead. In my years as a financial planner, I've always been surprised how many people are dumbfounded when I ask the following simple question:

"How much are your monthly nonhousing living expenses?"

This *should* be an easy question if you know where your money is going each month. The reality though is that most people get lost in the minutiae of their daily lives, and they really don't know how much they spend each month on coffee, lunches, gym memberships, or even gasoline. The next logical step in your personal finance journey is to build a budget and figure out where all your money goes each month. The good news is that building a budget is a low ETV activity perfect for the cold month of February.

One of the most popular budgeting plans is the 50/30/20 plan. This means that 50% of your after-tax income should go towards necessities, 30% towards "wants," and 20% towards debt and saving for retirement. The idea is that if someone follows this plan, and more importantly sticks to this plan over their lifetime, they will get out of debt, be able to retire comfortably, and most importantly still have room for fun and some indulgence. While I generally like this plan, I prefer a 50/25/25 plan. There is still plenty of room for "fun" in 25% of your income and allocating a little extra towards retirement and paying off debt is preferable over the long run. Just think of all the fun you will have when you get to retire early while your co-workers are still stuck in their cubicle at 65. Like in much of life, long-term planning and foresight are important to reach your goals.

The first step in building a budget is to separate your needs from your wants. This is where keeping and sticking to a budget gets tricky. The boundary between needs and wants is blurry, and it varies by person. I would go as far as to say many people think they *need* certain things, but they really are better characterized as wants. It might make you uncomfortable to give up something you enjoy, but that doesn't make it a necessity. If the budget process hurts, that means you are doing it right. Your needs should include the following:

- Groceries

- Utilities

- Insurance

- Housing

- Transportation

- Childcare and work expenses

If your needs are greater than 50% of your take-home income then you should consider dipping into the "wants" and "debt and saving" sections of your budget until you can reduce costs below 50%. Perhaps get a cheaper car payment, refinance your mortgage, switch to liability insurance, or rely on family instead of childcare service. The reality is that following a budget doesn't magically make your financial situation better. If you are living paycheck to paycheck and simply can't afford your basic needs, no amount of budgeting will solve that problem. I hope my advice can make your situation better, but sometimes there is only so much that can be done given your unique life circumstances. If your basic needs encompass 80% of your budget, then its ok to shift your other two categories down to 10% each, though I would always prioritize paying off high interest debt before entertainment spending or saving for retirement. Wants are bit more difficult to organize into a list because they tend to be highly personalized, so my list will likely not look like yours. Generally, all the following should be classified as wants:

- Travel and vacations

- Entertainment (TV, Netflix, movies, amusement parks, bars etc.)

- Gifts

- Dinners out, other food that goes beyond necessity (work lunches, organic food, etc.)

- Hobbies, collectibles, house décor, etc.

- Nonwork-related electronics

Things tend to get difficult in the wants category because many items that people view as necessary really are not. While it is certainly nice to have fancy work clothes, many people could probably get away with cheaper options. Other things like gym memberships and vehicles tend to be debatable. You might *need* a car to get to work, but an older high-mileage car might work fine and could save you a lot of money. The reality is that your car payment could be placed into both the needs and wants portion of a budget. I suggest budgeting the cost of basic transportation (e.g., the price of a used Toyota Corolla) into needs, and anything above that dollar amount into wants.

The final piece of the budget puzzle is our 25% towards debt repayment and retirement saving. This category is not much fun because it is hard to see the tangible benefit of paying off a debt for something you already have in your possession, or the usefulness of socking money away into a 401(k) that you won't touch for 30 years. I feel strongly that it is important for people to have fun with their money. Saving for retirement and sticking to a budget is going to be impossible if the journey to the end goal is unbearable. When I talk to my clients about their lives, I love to hear that they can spend time with their family, go on fun vacations, and enjoy their hobbies. Setting aside money each month to pay down debt and save for retirement should not make you so miserable you feel like you can't enjoy the important things that life has to offer. So, like in all things, budgeting is about balance. Try and allocate 25% to this category and see if you make it work without an adverse impact on your happiness, because more than anything else in our budget, allocating towards the future will reap huge benefits down the road. Is allocating 25% towards debt repayment and retirement saving too much? I don't think so, particularly if you want to retire before 65. Later in *Money Milestones,* I will outline the optimum order to contribute to your retirement accounts and to pay off debt. If you allocate a high percentage towards debt repayment and retirement early in your life, the effects are compounded, and in the end, you might not need to stick to 50/25/25 later in life. In other words, a large investment early might mean much more discretionary "fun money" later down the road. You can use some flexibility in this category, especially for unforeseen life events, emergencies, or unexpected expenses. But many people use that as an excuse to allocate less to saving, so it is important those deviations from the plan are only temporary!

The final obvious question to ask is how do you keep track of all this budget information? I use financial planning software to automate the process for my clients, but there are plenty of free options available to help you build your own budget. Many of these tools automatically calculate how much the user spends in different categories by syncing their bank and investment accounts and tracking their cash flow. For a simpler version of this, you could use a Microsoft Excel template or apps such as Personal Capital, Mint, or YNAB. Most of these apps track your progress and allow you to revisit your budget over time. We still have a long ten-month journey ahead, but I hope you are starting to see big picture ever so slightly starting to come into view. Building and following a budget is an important money milestone that will help you meet other major milestones as you progress. February is one of the coldest months in much of the United States, and it is the perfect time to begin the process of evaluating how much you spend on outdoor activities and taking some accountability to where your money goes each month.

Chapter 3

March:
There should never be surprises during tax season

Few things strike terror into the hearts of most Americans more than tax season. Whether it is the ever-looming threat of an audit, the hours spent staring at paperwork, or paying an expert only to learn that you owe money, it is generally an unpleasant time for most. Surely, you have heard the phrase "nothing is certain in life but death and taxes." This month I'd like to convince you that tax season (March–April) is an opportunity for you, and not something just to dread. Many people go through the motions each spring, but they miss small opportunities throughout the year to pay less in taxes when the bill comes due. So, we will discuss some tips that you can do to ensure you pay less. But even more important is the art of dodging tax land mines. History is filled with horror stories of simple, ordinary Americans making small mistakes that led to thousands of losses, including the loss of their livelihoods, businesses, and property. Apart from mistakes made during investment planning, tax mistakes have the most potential to single-handedly sabotage your financial future. Central to this issue is a simple question. Would you rather give the IRS a tax-free loan to hold your money all year, or would you rather have that money yourself?

According to *Forbes*, in 2008, Government Contractor Glen Wiggy made a significant tax mistake that led to an unexpected tax bill of $14,000 more than he anticipated.[6] He accepted a one-year position as an analyst in Iraq and was thrilled when his superiors told him his position was exempt from federal taxes. What they didn't tell him was that it was only exempt for a period of one year. He worked the position for *two* full years before he discovered that he was supposed to be paying federal taxes for the duration of the second year. He first recognized the error when his tax software told him he owed a bill of $15,000, when he was expecting a return of $1,000. Mr. Wiggy learned his lesson the hard way and had to cough up an additional $15,000 for his third year in Iraq as well, but this time he was at least armed with the knowledge so he could plan accordingly:

"Ever since, I've made it a priority to educate other government contractors and help them avoid the same horrible fate."

In a somewhat similar vein, a software engineer named Greg Simmonds and his wife, who worked as a freelancer, once hired a new tax professional to complete their taxes.[7] They were shocked to learn that they owed the IRS $7,000, when in past years, they had owed considerably less. At first, they were resigned to just pay the bill, but a nagging feeling that something wasn't right drove them to seek the insight of their family members. It turned out the tax professional had made a mistake in their property taxes, leading to a $5,000 balloon payment that had gone undetected by multiple people until it was eventually spotted by their parents! I'm sure you can see how simply putting the wrong number on a line could cost you thousands of dollars. As I researched these tax horror stories (and there are a shocking number of them), I noticed a central theme common to most of these situations. Many of these blunders can be caused by placing your blind trust about the details of federal tax code in someone else. What is it about tax planning that allows people the mental flexibility to just place their trust in the advice of their superior at work, their family, or even a professional?

For most people, taxes are a "black box." The metaphor, of course, refers to a system or object that can be viewed in terms of input and output (e.g., federal taxes in, refund checks out) without any knowledge of its internal workings. In our example, this means the implementation of the tax code is "opaque" or black. This simple fact is why most people tend to get in serious trouble with their taxes. The tax code is a complex labyrinth of rules, exceptions, exceptions to the rules, and even outright contradictions. The obvious tendency is to defer our tax decisions to another person. If that person is a CPA or other tax professional, that is probably a good thing. It is important to recognize experience and expert opinion. However, this can sometimes get people in trouble because filing your taxes is rarely a "one size fits all" endeavor. As a financial planner, I strongly recommend that everyone makes the effort to really understand the portion of the tax code that applies to their unique situation. I hear often from my clients that they "heard somewhere" about some tax loophole or situation that might apply to them. These situations are often ripe with exceptions that could lead people down the wrong path. So, the first step to good tax planning is to do the legwork to understand your situation, so you can effectively communicate with your CPA or tax professional. This is what I call the "land mine dodging" portion of tax planning. Nobody wants to be featured in an online article about "horrible tax disasters," and if you follow my advice, you never will!

Congratulations, you just got a new job. You put on your best new work clothes, bright-eyed and ready to start an exciting new career. Where is your first stop when you pull into work? Perhaps an exciting staff meeting with your co-workers? An important strategy discussion with your new boss? Maybe a welcome party in your honor? None of the above. It is a sad trip to human resources or the benefits office to complete your tax, insurance, and retirement paperwork. As boring as it might be, this meeting is an important part of your future financial situation. A small mistake here could lose you thousands of dollars over your lifetime. In March, we're focused on taxes, but in chapter eight (August), I'm going to tell you a tale of woe about how one decision I made in my employer's benefits office probably cost me $45,000 of investment earnings.

When I decided to write a chapter of *Money Milestones* on taxes, I thought to myself, *How the heck do I make taxes interesting?* I quickly realized that I could write hundreds of pages on specific situations related to tax planning, and all of the things that could go terribly wrong, depending on your income, employment status, changes to federal tax law, or any of a thousand different scenarios. But I think we can agree that is a boring proposition. I settled on two important components that I think everyone should know about taxes. First is "pay attention and avoid blowing yourself up" (discussed above). Second is, are your taxes set in stone each year? In other words, are there decisions that you can make that change your situation? Or is tax filing just an accounting exercise that is solved before you even start? I'd like to argue the former; there are many decisions you can make that drastically change your tax situation. Many people have the perception that their tax bill each year is chiseled into stone and an unchangeable result of their financial situation. Hopefully, I can convince you that you should carefully consider your tax decisions as you traverse the personal finance landscape.

Do you get a big juicy tax refund each spring? Do you look forward to that refund and plan major purchasing decisions around its arrival? What if I told you if you are getting a large refund check that you are making a poor financial planning decision? A big *refund* check is exactly that—a refund of your own money back to you. If you haven't been receiving that money in your paychecks throughout the year, that means you've been giving the U.S. Government a tax-free loan. My guess is that you probably don't want to give the government a tax-free loan, so why do so many people fall into this trap? The answer is that many folks use IRS tax withholding as "forced saving" device. That is, they don't have the willpower to save themselves, so they allow the government to use their money and "save" it for them, so they can receive as a lump sum the following year. Tax withholding is simply the portion of money your employer sets aside from your paychecks to cover your taxes. If you withhold too much, you loan the government your money and you will get a tax refund. If you withhold too little, the IRS sends you a bill. From a personal finance standpoint, the best option is to get as close to "$0" as possible. Why? Because of a concept called "time value of money" or TVM for short.

TVM means that your dollar today is worth more than a dollar in the future. This is because money can earn you interest throughout the year, either in investments like stocks and bonds (see chapter eight) or even in a high-yield savings account. In addition, inflation continually makes each dollar worth less as time goes on (about 2% less per year). According to IRS filing statistics, the average tax refund for the 2019 tax season was $2,725. If you get paid twice a month and receive the average refund, you should have had an extra $105 in every paycheck. Consider if you took that $2,725 and invested it throughout the year in the stock market. With a modest return of about 6%, contributing monthly, you would have about $2,800 by end of the year. This doesn't include inflation, which will make the difference even more dramatic. Obviously, this is not a lot of money for the average person, though it can be serious money for higher earners. But one of the benefits of following good personal finance habits is that many small differences throughout the year can add up to large differences over time. Regardless of the dollar amount, it will always be better to get access to your own money right away and become disciplined enough to invest and save wisely, as opposed to letting the government hold that money for you.

What other tips might we use to save on our taxes each year? They are numerous, but I'd like to mention a few that are "evergreen" tips. Evergreen plants leaf throughout the year, and the term is often used for business products or advice that stays relevant for a long period of time. Tax rules are ever-changing, so it is important that we only focus on things that are likely to always be relevant.

Tip #1: Always contribute to your retirement accounts if possible

Retirement accounts in this context are going to be work-sponsored plans (401(k)'s, 403(b)'s, etc.) or personal retirement accounts (IRAs). It can be quite easy to forget to make your IRA contribution each year, but make sure at a minimum you make your maximum contribution ($6,000 under 50 or $7,000 over 50 as of 2020). Ideally, this should be done with "new money" if you can afford it, but you can also shift funds from a taxable brokerage account if you have one. The primary benefit is a reduction in your taxable income each year. If you earn $50,000 per year but add $6,000 to an IRA and $8,000 to your 401(k), your taxable income is only $36,000 (not counting other considerations). The net result is that you pay less taxes and save for retirement, all while earning the same amount you would normally. Consider the following alternative: instead of saving $6,000 in an IRA, you instead put that money in your checking account. In this scenario, you must pay taxes on that $6,000 first, but if it's in an IRA, you get to deduct it from your taxable earnings. The take-home point is: if you can save long term, keep that money in a tax-advantaged retirement account, not in your bank account (assuming you already have an emergency fund). You will pay less taxes and thank yourself when you are older.

Tip #2: Itemize your deductions

Most people doing their taxes take the standard deduction and go along their merry way. It is easy and simple. However, there is still a large segment of the population that would benefit from itemizing their deductions, so it is worth the effort to work through calculating your itemized costs. Families that own expensive homes in high tax areas have paid a large amount of medical and dental bills, own a lot of real estate, or have made large donations to charity are likely to come out ahead by itemizing. It can be a painful process, but there is good reason to always make the comparison between the itemized and standard deduction before deciding which way to go.

Some of the most common itemized deductions are:

• Home mortgage interest

• Property, state, and local income taxes

• Investment interest expense

• Medical expenses

• Charitable contributions

• Miscellaneous deductions

Tip #3: Always file electronically

Firstly, if you are expecting a tax refund, why would you not want access to your funds earlier? The IRS processes electronically filed returns three to six weeks faster than paper returns. As discussed earlier, the time value of money concept suggests that the earlier you get access to money, the higher its future value is (i.e., it can start earning interest earlier). Even if you don't expect a refund, it is still best to file electronically because (according to Turbo Tax), less than 1% of electronically filed returns have errors, whereas nearly 20% of paper returns have errors (or more commonly omissions).[8] There are also better records (digital receipts) for filers to prove when and where they filed their returns. If your return is lost by the postal service, you might not be able to prove it arrived at the IRS in a timely manner and would therefore incur additional interest and penalties for late filing.

Tip #4: Communicate with your dependents near tax time

Make sure to record the Taxpayer Identification Numbers (usually Social Security Numbers) for your children and any other dependents on your return. This is important because the IRS won't allow any dependent credits that you might be entitled to, such as the Child Tax Credit. A child can only be claimed as a dependent by one parent unless you are married and filing jointly. If you are a single filer, this requires that the child doesn't provide more than half of their own financial support and resides with you for more than half the tax year. This only applies to dependents under the age of 19 or under the age of 24 if they are attending school in a full-time capacity. Therefore, it is extremely important that you communicate with your spouse (or ex-spouse if you are divorced) to coordinate who is claiming the dependent, and even more importantly if the dependent should claim themselves.

I hope by now you see that tax season is ripe with opportunities to help you in your personal finance journey. If you can avoid the "land mines," get access to your money before Uncle Sam does, and follow a few general tips, you will be on your way to never being surprised during tax season.

Chapter 4

April:
Keep your friends close and your enemies closer

There are many central principles that allow modern societies to flourish and grow into robust economies with high standards of living, plentiful resources, and happy citizens. Perhaps most central to the growth of modern society is simply trust. That is, the fact that millions of people can hold similar beliefs about the world, make business deals, integrate into society, and generally cooperate amongst each other is largely because of trust. This is because the default position for most people is to believe what they are told, from the media, government departments, businesses, employers, and other public institutions. The notion that public figures and professionals are trustworthy has been integral to the health of representative democracies. After all, one of the central tenants of democratic governments is that a small group of people (politicians) can represent thousands or even millions of others. The cynics among you are probably rolling your eyes, since according to the Pew Research Center, public trust in the government has been declining since the 1960s, with only 17% of Americans today saying they can trust the government in Washington to do what is right "just about always" (3%) or "most of the time" (14%).[9] However, consider your feelings of trust at the individual level, where you are interacting with a single person at a business establishment or other public institution. Most people tend to trust others as individuals when they are sharing pieces of information with each other. The presumption is that their intentions are honest. Consider your default assumptions when discussing information with your doctor, lawyer, teacher, co-worker, waiter, cashier, or neighbor. Most of us operate under the default position that those people are being honest with us when we are sharing information. It might be hard to believe given the conspiracy theories running rampant about climate change, vaccines, and the coronavirus, but according to a survey by NORC (The University of Chicago), trust in scientists and doctors has actually held steady since the 1970s, even increasing the past decade.[10] Many fringe ideas are given more promotion these days, but generally trust is still high for professionals. As for financial professionals, the question of trust can be incredibly complicated. Financial professionals are in the unique position to hold the intimate details of their client's wealth, and presumably, that comes with trusted advice that is in the best interest of their client. But is that always the case? Sadly, the answer is that *some* financial professionals have their client's best interest in mind but others do not. In 2004, the U.S. Senate recognized April as "Financial Literacy Month," with many financial organizations doing promotions and education outreach during April. Those very same financial organizations are best positioned to promote good financial literacy to the public during April. But can you trust them? We're going to celebrate Financial Literacy Month by discussing which providers of financial advice you can trust, and which you can't.

Far too often in the business world, the consumer seems to be taken advantage of. Companies track the websites you visit, your social media, spending patterns, credit card use, and even your place of business. All of us are trained from childhood to withstand the constant barrage of advertising trying to get a small slice of our income. The advertising stream just becomes part of our lives, almost a "white noise" in the background that we learn to tune out. But that is mostly for product-based businesses. Generally, when considering professional service-based business (legal, financial, medical, etc.) we depend on referrals or do significantly more research into the company before deciding. There is simply more at stake when you are considering the legal expertise of your attorney as opposed to which brand of ice cream is the best choice for dessert. When considering who should best run their investment portfolio or help with retirement planning, the average person might search for a "financial advisor." Or possibly a "wealth manager," "financial consultant," "financial planner," "investment advisor," "investment manager," "fiduciary," or "financial coach." Do those terms even mean anything? How is the average person supposed to figure out how they are different? Or which letters after someone's name are the best: CFA, CFP, ChFC, CIMA, CMT, CIC, CFS, and so on. Consider the list of titles again:

- Financial Advisor

- Wealth Manager

- Financial Consultant

- Financial Planner

- Investment Advisor

- Investment Manager

- Fiduciary

- Financial Coach

Only two of these titles mean anything. Can you guess which two? Fiduciary and Investment Advisor, specifically a Registered

Investment Advisor (RIA). The rest can be used by anybody and have no intrinsic meaning. This is most egregiously abused by the insurance industry. Insurance agents selling predatory, high-fee annuities and life insurance policies call themselves "financial advisors" when really, they are insurance salespeople. This practice is confusing to the consumer, and frankly, should be illegal. As a short aside, there is never a good reason to invest with an insurance company. Their products have massive hidden fees, make enormous commissions off your account, and force you into predatory contracts that are difficult to escape. Term-life insurance is important for your family's financial plan (see "November," chapter 11), but investment products combined with life insurance (annuities, whole, universal life) are almost always a terrible deal. Even your local bank is not a safe haven because many bank salespeople have a specific agenda in mind when you meet with them to discuss your finances. They want to sell you a product. Most often, it is a specific fund that your bank receives commissions to place your money into. Unfortunately, the same is true for many popular broker-dealers around the U.S., whose names seem to commonly be male first names. Many of these companies sell you a "branded" product (often a mutual fund) that has enormous fees and commissions, when alternative products are identical but with much lower costs. Would you pay $100 for a brand-name medicine, when the generic tablet is identical and only $10? The problem with many banks, broker-dealers, and insurance companies is that they are not on the same side as you. That means that they receive a cut of your money (via commissions, "load" costs, or annuity fees) no matter what happens. Once they "sell" you the fund, they get paid, even if that fund is not the best fit for your needs. As you can probably imagine, the funds that pay the "financial advisor" the most are always going to be the best for you. What a coincidence!

In contrast, a "fiduciary" or a Registered Investment Advisor (RIA) is often not affiliated with a broker and receives nothing by putting you into specific funds. In other words, they are on the "same side" as you. The concept of a "fiduciary" can be applied to a lot of situations, as it generally means a person who acts on behalf of another person to manage assets. Essentially, a fiduciary is a person or organization that owes to another the duties of good faith and trust. They can be board members, the trustee of a trust or estate, or even an attorney to a client. If your money is with a Registered Investment Advisor who has no vested interest in selling the products of a specific brokerage company, they can fulfill their fiduciary responsibility to you when choosing investments. Generally, that means charging a small flat percentage fee annually. As the value of your assets goes up, their fee goes up. In contrast, broker-dealers, who are often compensated by commission, only must fulfill what is called a "suitability obligation," which means making recommendations that are somewhat consistent with the best interests of their client. Instead of having to place the clients' interests above their own, the suitability standard only details that the broker-dealer must reasonably believe the recommendations are somewhat suitable for the clients' financial needs, outlook, and risk assessment.

As you can imagine, this means that when you see a "financial advisor" at a bank or broker-dealer chain, they have an incentive to place your money in funds that benefit them the most, not you. Let's just consider a simple example that shows the scale of financial loss that most people are susceptible to when they invest in non-fiduciary companies. Kaylie and her husband, Jack, have been in the workforce for about ten years after graduating from college. They have scrimped and saved and are ready to open IRAs and a brokerage account with the $100,000 they have in their bank account. They logically think the best place to start is with their local bank and broker: Eddie James

Company. They chat with the "financial advisor" at the bank, and he happily agrees to set up their investment accounts. Their financial advisor is required to place all new clients into Eddie James Company's branded mutual funds. He receives a nice commission for doing so, often a few percent of the total purchase price. Further, the Eddie James Co mutual funds have a "front-load" cost of 5%. That means that the company receives 5% of Kaylie and Jack's $100,000 deposit immediately. Then, they are charged a 1.50% advising fee each year. Kaylie and Jack are excited to be building wealth for their future, and they agree to deposit an additional $1,000 per month into their investment accounts, each time paying a front-load cost of 5%.

Let's flash-forward 25 years into Kaylie and Jack's future. They have kept to their plan and deposited $1,000 per month with Eddie James Co for 25 years, adding to their initial deposit of $100,000. They are now in their late 50s and think they are ready to retire a bit early, do some traveling, and have some freedom from the daily grind of their office jobs. So how did their Eddie James account do after 25 years assuming they received on average a 7% annual return? Kaylie and Jack contributed $400,000 of their own money, and after 25 years of growth, ended up with $940,663 (Table 1). Sounds great, right? Until you realize that they paid a total of $350,175 in fees. Their total balance without fees is $1,290,839. That is an enormous amount of money they paid Eddie James in fees, load costs, and commissions. Now consider an alternative scenario, where instead Kaylie and Jack did a bit more research and found a reasonably priced Registered Investment Advisory (RIA) company to instead act as their financial planner for the next 25 years. If they did their due diligence, Kaylie and Jack could easily find a company that doesn't use load cost funds, doesn't take commissions, and instead only charges a reasonable flat percentage fee each year, like 0.9%. Flash-forward 25 years, and now their investment accounts have a balance of $1,113,417. Kaylie and Jack now have an extra $172,754 to use during retirement because they went with a low-cost fiduciary instead of a predatory bank or a broker. This is a massive amount of money and can easily be the difference between reaching your goals and struggling in your later years. If they instead had invested with an insurance company, their returns would be even worse.

Bank or broker with commissions	Total contribution:	$385,000.00
	Total Balance without Fees:	$1,290,839.11
	Total Fees:	$350,175.83
	Total Balance with Fees:	**$940,663.28**
Low-fee fiduciary	Total contribution	$400,000.00
	Total Balance without Fees:	$1,330,212.58
	Total Fees:	$216,794.97
	Total Balance with Fees:	**$1,113,417.61**

Table 1. Kaylie and Jack's wealth over their lifetime when using a fiduciary vs a commission based broker.

As we can see from Table 1, your choice of who manages your money is important. The reality is that fees are an important component of your investment performance over time. Most banks and brokers do not offer "special" funds that perform better than cheaper options. The reality is that they often perform worse. For example, why would you pay extra for a bank or broker branded S&P 500 stock fund, when the same fund is available in a cheaper variety? They both hold assets in the same companies at the same proportions. As I noted earlier, a good analogy is generic vs "brand-name" medicine with the exact same active ingredients. They are identical, so you are paying for nothing and essentially "donating" your money to a for-profit business for no added benefit. In this case, it can lose you hundreds of thousands of dollars over your lifetime. It is tempting to think "Well, I'll just manage my money myself" when you look at a fee breakdown like this. However, good fiduciary advisors will earn their fee and help you make money over time, you just need to make sure you are paying a reasonable fee for that service.

It might seem contradictory that I'm criticizing the fees charged by the financial industry and suggesting you work with a professional to manage your investments. The reality is that most people lose far more money when they attempt to run their own investment accounts. If the fee is reasonable and you find a fiduciary you trust, the benefits can be huge. So how do they help you grow your money better? Firstly, they help you avoid small mistakes that can lose you thousands over time. These small "invisible" losses include things like choosing the wrong funds, investing too conservatively, not placing the correct type of investment inside and outside an IRA (see "August," chapter eight for more), overpaying taxes, not rebalancing portfolios properly, and a host of other small mistakes. These add up over time and will result in major losses. A good fiduciary will account for these small-scale losses and help limit them over time, particularly if they are independent and not obligated to sell specific funds. It probably comes as no surprise to most that it is much easier to see faults with others than it is with ourselves. Fiduciary financial planners provide a neutral and experienced third party to give unbiased advice on your financial decision-making. They also hold you accountable to change those poor decision-making habits. Most of us are not particularly good at keeping ourselves accountable to our decisions but find it much easier with someone else helping to steer the boat. I give all my clients "tasks" to complete between financial planning meetings to keep them on track and accountable. By far the most dramatic impact a good advisor can have on your wealth is behavioral in nature. There is a plethora of investing biases people hold, or even worse, behavioral mistakes they make, which lead to general underperformance compared to professional advisors. This underperformance is fueled by poor decision-making and impulsivity, which causes annual difference of around 2% which can cost hundreds of thousands of dollars over a lifetime.[11] Fiduciary planners act as behavioral coaches and encourage people to not panic at the wrong times, to stick to their investment plans, and they help their clients deal with the emotional aspects of losing money. They also use more sophisticated rebalancing techniques, maximize tax losses (tax-loss harvesting), and use other tricks to maximize return over time. History is filled with "do-it-yourselfers" that accidentally stuck themselves with enormous tax bills they couldn't pay (the "land mines" we discussed in the previous chapter). Your fiduciary is intimately aware of the tax considerations involved with your investments.

Our last consideration for financial literacy month is to discuss *how* to rigorously evaluate potential financial advisors. Above, we discussed *why* they are important to help you grow your wealth, but many of them are not your friends. First, consider a blanket set of questions you should ask your potential candidates:

- How much is your fee and how frequently is it assessed?

- What is your educational background, and what certifications do you hold?

- What is your previous professional experience?

- Do you receive larger commissions for certain types of investments?

- Do you carry liability insurance?

- Can you provide a list of references of existing clients in a financial situation like mine?

- What additional financial planning services will you provide me with?

- What are my options if I'm dissatisfied with your service?

If you would like this simplified even further, here is my recommended flowchart for making this important decision:

1. Are you affiliated with a bank or insurance company? (*If yes, run away; if no, go to question #2*).

2. Do you receive any commissions for the sale of investment products? (*If yes, run away; if no, go to question #3*).

3. Is the combined advising fee + fund fee more than 1%? (*If yes, run away; if no, go to question #4*).

4. Are you a registered fiduciary that is independent and not affiliated with a specific broker? (*If yes, go to question #5*).

5. Can you produce references of clients in similar financial positions as me? (*If yes and they are good references, go to question #6*).

6. Do you feel like you can trust this person to make good decisions on your behalf with only your best interest in mind? (*If yes, move to #7*).

7. You should consider hiring this person and their company.

Chapter 5

May:

Do you know where your money is going?

In June of 2014, the small town of Brattleboro, Vermont, was shocked to learn that 92-year-old Ronald Read had left six million dollars upon his death to the town library and Battleboro Memorial Hospital.[12] Why was this so shocking? Mr. Read had spent his entire career as a janitor and gas station attendant and quietly amassed a fortune of eight million dollars, without even his family's knowledge. Read came from very humble beginnings. He was the first in his family to graduate from high school and served in the military extensively during World War II. Later, he became married, had two children with his wife, and spent decades working at a gas station and as a janitor at JCPenney. He spent his entire life living as frugal as possible, driving older used cars, repairing his clothes instead of buying new ones, and doing as much yardwork and housework as possible himself, even into his 90s. Instead of spending his money on a lavish lifestyle, he put as much of his wealth as possible into the stock market, having the discipline to hold his positions for decades, like investing legend Warren Buffet. Investing in this way is not something most people have the foresight and patience for, which is why I generally recommend using an advisor to help keep you focused. But Mr. Read had extraordinary patience and vision, even with a low salary and what many would consider undesirable jobs. What is shocking about this story is not that Mr. Read accumulated eight million dollars during a 92-year lifetime, but that he did so while raising a family and working low-paying jobs. This reveals an important concept in our personal finance journey. You don't need a huge paycheck to become rich, in fact, you just need discipline and a plan that works. Of course, it is probably more fun to get rich by inheriting a giant trust fund from your uncle at 25. But that is not realistic for most people and hoping to strike it rich isn't a solid financial plan. Even if you are a low earner, it is possible to generate wealth by minimizing costs throughout your lifetime and subsequently investing that money. This is only possible if you are able to avoid the relentless advances of lifestyle creep, constant upgrades, excessive subscriptions, and over-priced food. All these small charges and subscriptions will eat away at your checking account each month like a plague and leave you with little to no financial security in the future. May is the perfect month to broach this issue, because as the weather turns nicer, many people start to become more active, go out to restaurants, hit-up bars, and become "freer" with their money than they would have during the winter. I do not want to shame anybody for enjoying their life, but it is important to understand your long-term goals and if your current spending habits are getting in the way of those goals. Will you be Ronald Read? Or just another person living paycheck to paycheck without any hope of escape? Believe it or not, our story starts with coffee.

In 2008, I was working on my Ph.D. at the University of Oklahoma. My wife and I had recently gotten married, and our budget was pretty tight. Graduate students do not get paid much (around $20,000/year), and my wife was in a transitionary period and had reluctantly accepted a museum position for $9/hour. Our basic needs were covered, but we certainly did not start earning a good income until a few years later when both of our careers had progressed. Undaunted by our financial position, I remained committed to start my day at Starbucks with a coffee and a pastry. I'll admit it now, I have a Starbucks problem, and it has taken years for me to cut back my consumption. Obviously, we knew how much money my food cost each day when I purchased it, but it wasn't until we sat down and took a seriously hard look at where our money was going that we realized the extent of the spending. On average, I was spending about $4 per day on my coffee and breakfast. Seems innocent enough. But that is $20 a week, or $1,040 per year. Throw in the occasional lunches, gas station snacks, or energy drinks, and now we're talking about $2,500 per year. Again, not too much if your household income is $250,000 year, but if you are in graduate school and making $35,000 per year, it becomes more than 7% of your total yearly income! We developed a game plan to break the reliance on Starbucks and other trips to morning coffee shops. I would wake up 15 minutes earlier and make my own coffee and breakfast at home. It is a simple lifestyle change, and it freed some cash to make our lives easier in a period where we were struggling financially. The trick is to realize that "improvements" to your budget need to be lifestyle changes, not impulsive decisions that you will backtrack on a few weeks later. Just like losing weight requires discipline and lifestyle change, and not a fad diet, financial choices should be made with a permanent change in mind. It will hurt temporarily to bring a sad packed lunch to work instead of going to the local restaurant every day, but guess what? Eventually, it just becomes part of your new routine and you get used to it. Then, when you do splurge on a nice work lunch or breakfast, it will feel more rewarding because you understand this is a reward for sticking to your financial lifestyle change.

Let's start with the obvious facts: Yes, you will obviously save money by making your coffee at home rather than buying it before work. You will always save money by preparing food at home, utilizing leftovers, or meal prepping throughout the week. But how much? This is where it becomes jaw-dropping. Depending on where you live and how fancy you prefer your coffee drinks, you are likely spending between $1 and $5 per cup. Meanwhile, brewing coffee at home costs you between 16 and 18 cents per cup. In our home, that means that I now spend about $42 per year instead of $1,040. And this is just coffee! We have not talked about dinner, subscriptions, gym costs, beauty/grooming services, or any of the other ways that our money is slowly sucked out of our grasp each month.

There is one more unresolved question related to the coffee conundrum. What do I do with the $1,000 I saved by making the "coffee at home" lifestyle choice? Ronald Read was so successful because he invested the money he saved by making frugal lifestyle choices. Let's say I stick to the "coffee at home" plan and instead invest that $1,000 into an IRA, and it receives an average market return of 7%. Next year, I have $1,070, but then I add to that an additional $1,000 from my annual coffee savings. If I invested that coffee money monthly and kept to the plan for 20 years, my total IRA balance would be $43,489. Alternatively, if I kept buying coffee every day, I would have a negative $20,000 loss over 20 years, likely more because of inflation. This is how you generate wealth if you do not have a high salary. It works, but it takes commitment and sacrifice.

Coffee and daily snacks are only one piece of a much larger puzzle that is your annual spending. Hopefully, by now, you are starting to see that minor expenses + time = major expenses. When the cash saved from those major expenses is invested, it then turns into serious wealth that your future self will appreciate. What are some other areas where these small insidious charges are eating away at your budget? One of the most obvious is your subscriptions. This could include monthly gym subscriptions, streaming services (Netflix, Hulu, Disney+, etc.), audio services like Spotify, pre-packaged food delivery, mobile apps with monthly subscriptions, e-book and magazine subscriptions, and software. Even Amazon will try and rope you into regular monthly charges for common household items. Have you ever considered why companies like the subscription model so much? It is because they know most people will take the path of least resistance and leave their subscription active long after they need it! Do you really need to pay $10 per month for that app that can identify insects in your backyard? The first step to breaking this cycle is to do a complete audit of all the charges being processed each month. Many services might have you on annual subscription, and it can be even harder to remember about those until it is too late, and you end up paying another year for something you no longer needed. The next step is to communicate with the rest of your family and/or household to make sure *everyone* is doing the same audit with their accounts and to confirm that the subscriptions are no longer being used. Then it is time to make some decisions. Which subscriptions are you going to cancel, and what is your approach for replacing that service with a cheaper option? For example, consider alternating your streaming services every few months, and only keeping one active at a time. Use free pick-up service or in-store shopping for groceries instead of expensive subscriptions to pre-made dinner services. Finally, come up with a schedule to regularly audit all your subscriptions. At least once a year, your entire household should reconsider which services are regularly being used and are necessary, and which can be removed. As a thought experiment, try taking a long-term approach to consider if you should subscribe to a service. In other words, instead of thinking "Do I want to pay $15/month for this?"

frame your thought process as "Would I be willing to pay $540 to have access to this for the next three years?" This will help you keep some perspective on the long-term consequences of that subscription. Consider how your $540 would have grown over three years if it had instead been invested and was earning a return.

Why do so many people fall into the trap of slowly losing their wealth to tiny transactions, invisible purchases, and account draining subscriptions? I believe there are four primary causes for why this happens to so many middle-class Americans: 1) inefficiency and thirst for convenience, 2) lack of creative problem solving, 3) not embracing what you already have, and 4) the belief that "it is only money." Many of the small purchases we make are because of convenience. Buying coffee is easier than making it. Same with lunch. Paying someone to mow your lawn is much more convenient than doing it yourself on your day off. Subscriptions are similar in that we are often paying a premium to avoid some type of activity. Don't want to shop for groceries? Blue Apron, Freshly, and EveryPlate will deliver dinner packages directly to you each week. But you will pay a hefty fee for that convenience. Instead of focusing on trying to make your life easier by paying for it, consider trying to be more efficient with your time and daily routine. Consolidate your trips, make more detailed schedules, wake up 15 minutes earlier, and hold yourself accountable for your time! The solution to the convenience problem is time, not money. My guess is that when you read "lack of creative problem solving" earlier, it wasn't immediately apparent how that could possibly help you save money each month. Most people do not immediately try and maximize and reuse the physical items in their house. We are afraid of being called hoarders, and most folks like to keep their houses clean and without clutter. I get it, I'm one of those people. My default position is to throw out anything that is not being used to keep the house decluttered. But my wife is a master at reusing items and always comes up with creative ways to repurpose items to solve a problem. Recently, I lamented the lack of shipping materials we had available for some items we were planning on selling online. I proposed bubble wrap or packing peanuts; it was only $15 after all. She proposed saving our egg cartons, granola bar boxes, and fruit cartons to use as insulation in our shipping boxes. It was completely free and worked great. We are lucky enough to have a large wild blackberry patch growing in our backyard. We pick the blackberries every summer, but if conditions get dry, the harvest is dismal. I proposed buying an extra-long second water hose with an adapter to run water to the wild blackberries. My wife proposed saving water and milk gallons all year long so we could easily transport 20 gallons to our backyard. Is it less convenient than 100 feet of hose? Yes. Is it more work? Absolutely. But it is a 100% free solution to a simple problem we had.

Have you ever stopped and really thought about how items are marketed to you? There is an underlying theme of FOMO (Fear of Missing Out) present in most marketing campaigns. These campaigns want you to believe that your phone is terrible and does not have the newest facial recognition and camera features. You should feel bad. You are missing out and are not part of the technological revolution. Marketing campaigns of a variety of different types (media, technology, clothes/fashion) all push a similar agenda on their audience: making you feel bad for not having the latest and greatest items. But the reality is that most of the time, the upgrades are only very minor. An iPhone one or two generations ago does *most* of the same functions as the newest model. It is important to learn to be grateful for what you have and only upgrade when it is necessary. This is particularly important for younger people that might feel pressure to have the trendiest items. My favorite example of unnecessary upgrades is golf clubs. Golf club manufacturers learned more than 15 years ago how to make clubs both light and larger for more forgiving hitting area. The truth is that there is very little that you can do to improve the performance of a driver when its already made of superlight material and is so large that you "can't miss." So how do they market their new products each year? Mostly with buzz words that sound super advanced: "airfoil technology," "gravity core," "dispersion," and "speed pocket." People spend $450 on new drivers (that is only for *one* club if you are not familiar with golf) because they fall into the trap of wanting something better, when what they have is 99% as effective as a newer model.

Finally, all too often I hear people rely on a simple phrase to justify their spending "it is only money." I think this phrase is dangerous. Not because money is the most important thing in life (of course, it is not) but because money allows your family to reach their goals and live the life they desire. That is far more important than the money itself. The money is just a tool to help you be secure and live a fulfilling life. When you waste it frivolously, you only end up borrowing from your own future. Many of my suggestions in this chapter might seem very minor to you (make coffee at home, reuse household items), but it is probably much harder to implement than you realize. They require a lifestyle change and sacrifice. For those of us firmly entrenched in the middle class, sacrifice is required to build wealth. Ronald Read worked his entire life with a low income and still became wealthy. You can too if you are willing to make some small sacrifices.

Chapter 6

June:
Is your house an investment?

In most years, June is the month with both the highest number of house sales and the highest median sales price.[13] The early summer is a great time to be both a buyer and seller, as there are many properties available and the seller premium is high. Summer brings a lot of competition into the market since many people are looking to settle into new jobs and relocate their family before school starts in September. Many people do not have the convenience of choosing when they need to sell their home and buy another, but the relative timing of these purchases could make a massive difference in your long-term financial position. For most families, their primary residence is the largest purchase they will ever make in their lifetime. The decision will reverberate into the future and can have great rewards or significant consequences. Therefore, it is important to not be impulsive and really study the financial implications of your decision. There is more to the choice than "Are there good schools nearby?" "How new is the roof?" and "Does it have a nice backyard?" This month we will explore how you should approach your property purchase, and where to place your residence in your financial plan. If it is the largest purchase you will ever make, surely it counts as an investment, right? Shockingly, we have made it all the way to June, and we have not even defined an "investment" yet. The answer, like many things in life, is a bit nebulous.

In most areas of the country, the best time of the year to sell a home is in May and June. Houses sell nearly 19 days faster than average and for a shocking 6% increase in sale price.[14] What does that mean for the buyer? Obviously, the buyer is the one that pays the "seller premium" for the thriving housing market in the late spring and early summer. In other words, if you are not exceptionally picky about your needs for your home, you stand to save a significant amount of money by making your offers during more off-peak times of the year, such as the late fall and early winter. This 6% savings has a compounding effect through time since most people take out a mortgage with interest to pay off their home. Consider the following two scenarios:

- Sally purchases a home for $250,000 in June with a 3% 30-year mortgage. Her total lifetime cost = $379,444.

- Sally purchases a home for $235,000 in December (6% less) with a 3% 30-year mortgage. Her total lifetime cost = $356,677.

Sally saved a total of $22,767 just by making a strategic choice about when she purchased a home. She likely had to make some sacrifices, as her options for available houses will be slimmer in the winter, but if she is not picky, this is a massive amount of savings for no real effort. But we're not done yet. There are a host of other smaller decisions that you can make to generate big savings in the future.

In the 1950s, a real estate attorney named Max Karl started a mortgage company that specialized in a new product they called private mortgage insurance (PMI). Unlike many mortgage insurers who collapsed during the Great Depression, his company only insured the first 20% of losses on a mortgage where the owner defaulted. This protected the insurance company more than previous forms of mortgage insurance and led to a boom in banks and other lenders providing more loans to buyers whose down payments were less than 20% of the home's price. Over the next 30 years, PMI became mandatory on most mortgages, and the only way to waive the fee was to put 20% down on the house at the time of purchase. In other words, if buyers today do not put 20% down on a new mortgage, they must pay a monthly fee for the lifetime of the loan. This fee protects the lender, not you! More specifically, it protects the lender *from* you. Buyers that can't put 20% down on their mortgage are deemed riskier by the lender with a higher probability of default. PMI can lead to massive losses over decades, so my next piece of advice is to make sure you always put 20% down. Let's check in with Sally again:

- Sally purchases a home for $300,000, with a 3% 30-year mortgage. She puts $0 down and pays PMI of 0.75%. Her total lifetime cost = $497,381.

- Sally purchases a home for $300,000 with a 3% 30-year mortgage. This time she puts down 20% and pays no PMI. Her total lifetime cost = $405,554.90

Now imagine if Sally combines her savings by buying at the right time of year and puts down 20% to remove PMI. The lifetime savings are extraordinary. But there is one more piece to the puzzle that will allow Sally, our intrepid homebuyer, to save even more.

It is not surprising to most people that real estate agents take a nice big slice out of your home sale as a commission, usually around 6%. Losing $18,000 on $300,000 can feel like a slap in the face, especially if your house languished on the market for months, or even years. Surprising, I'm not going to argue that you sell your house yourself (for sale by owner), because there are studies that show that owners receive lower sale prices than agents.[15] However, there are still some import-ant aspects to finding the right real estate agent for you. Notice that I said the *right* agent for *you*. In other words, there is a performance history that you can research for different agents as well as agents that specialize in certain areas, types of homes, or even have regular clientele that purchase investment properties. I highly recommend doing your due diligence when starting the process. Secondly, remember that 6% commission is just an average amount that agents charge, and it needs to be split between both the buying and selling agent, and their parent broker (basically the management branch for the transaction). Even so, many agents are willing to negotiate and reduce their commission, particularly in areas where houses sell quickly or if you are willing to lose some services (such as open houses). A negotiated drop of 1% is still a few thousand dollars back in your pocket or money that you can use for upgrades to your new home. I know that many people view negotiation in a negative context or as unnecessarily confrontational, but there many examples in personal finance where you will benefit for being your own advocate.

Everyone has heard the story of someone's parents or grandpar-ents that bought a house in the 1960s or 1970s for $15,000, and then sold it in 2020 for 1.2 million. It is easy to assume that a house is an investment if the real estate market is driving home prices upwards consistently over time. However, this is an extremely contentious issue in the financial planning world. Some experts say houses are not invest-ments, others consider them your most important long-term invest-ment. Finance nerds have argued until red in the face for one side or the other, and you can read many articles online taking different posi-tions. Before I gave you *this* finance nerd's opinion, I need to define a few other simple concepts first.

Have you ever considered where Jeff Bezos or Bill Gates keeps all his money? The media is always talking about the "net worth" of the rich and famous, but where is that money stored? The reality is that most of the ultra-wealthy don't have billions lying around, because their wealth is tied up into *assets*. Assets are resources that store value. Stocks, bonds, and cash are assets; your home or other property is an asset, even that collection of *Star Wars* figures in your basement can be considered an asset. At the time I write this, Jeff Bezos has a net worth of 196 billion dollars. But that money is not just sitting in his checking account, it's mostly stored in Amazon stock, property, and business assets. Your assets (while not as extensive as Mr. Bezos') likely include your cash, retirement, and investment accounts, property, vehicles, and other household goods. Unfortunately, if assets are the "light side" of the net worth equation, *liabilities* are the "dark side". Liabilities are debt, and when calculating your net worth, it needs to be subtracted from your assets:

Net Worth = Assets – Liabilities

According to Experian, the average American in 2019 has $90,460 in personal debt.[16] The most common debt liabilities for Americans include car loans, credit cards, student loans, and of course, mortgages. Just like compound interest generates wealth, the interest on your liabilities has an opposite effect, growing rapidly and eroding your net worth. As you have probably surmised, if your house is an asset then the corresponding mortgage is the liability portion of that equation. If your home is worth more than you owe, you have built *homeowner's equity*, which helps build your net worth. Since your home equity tends to build over time, many people believe houses are investments, but the boundaries are blurry.

An investment is broadly defined as an "asset purchased with the idea that will provide income in the future or be sold later at a higher price for a profit." If I buy bonds, I might receive a monthly interest payment for as long as I hold that bond. If I start a business for $50,000, but later that business provides an income of $100,000/year, that is clearly an investment that paid off. Similarly, company stock can be purchased for one price and sold later for a much higher (or lower!) price. Even toys and collectibles can be shockingly good investments. LEGO sets have appreciated in value better than some traditional investments like gold, stocks, and bonds, yielding an average return of about 11% from 1987 to 2015 according to recent economic studies.[17] Recently, a LEGO Captain America and Iron Man set released in 2012 was sold at an auction for $11,200! These are all assets that generate either income or monetary gains in the future. On the surface, it seems that your residence fits the definition, since most houses do appreciate over time.

The primary reason people purchase a home is for shelter. Your home is a residence that you build your life around, and as such, requires a significant amount of "upkeep" and maintenance over time. Not only do you have to make monthly mortgage payments, but you also must pay real estate taxes, homeowners' insurance, sometimes private mortgage insurance (PMI), and utilities. You pay to maintain the property, which means providing repairs and general maintenance, as necessary. These ongoing expenses are called *carrying costs*—the costs of holding the asset over time. Repairs associated with being a homeowner can also be significant. Replacing a roof, gutters, siding and doors, remodeling kitchens and bathrooms can be expensive. In 2020, the average cost of replacing a heating, ventilation, and air conditioning unit (HVAC) in the U.S. was $5,750, and the average cost of draining a septic tank about $400. Many personal finance gurus and financial planners have made the case that these carrying costs add up over time, and the result is that even though it feels like you made money when you sold your house, the reality is that you did not. In other words, a home is an asset that has ongoing liabilities associated with it, and when you sum up the liabilities upon the house sale, they might negate your proceeds from the sale.

I understand the logic of these arguments, but I do think that houses can be good investments. Alternatively, they can also be a black hole of endless carrying costs. In other words, there is no "once size fits all" answer to "Are houses investments?" Some houses are going to appreciate much more than their ongoing costs, especially if they are in growing areas with good schools, and others might lead to thousands of dollars in losses by the time they are sold. So, just like some company stock is a good investment over time, and others go bankrupt, houses are similar. There is one final piece of this puzzle that I think most people seem to forget when they argue that houses are not investments. You do not have to pay rent when you own a home! Rent in this scenario is called an *opportunity cost*. Opportunity costs are the loss of potential gains when one alternative is chosen. In other words, when you choose to rent instead of paying a mortgage, you "lose" the gain in equity that you would be receiving by paying off a home. When we factor this back into the equation, many homes become good investments. However, this is highly dependent on location, rental costs, the housing market, and many other factors. But just like stock, there is an element of risk, and many homebuyers will make poor decisions that will lead to them losing money on their primary home.

In 2008, the financial world was rocked by the housing crisis, an event so incredible it almost brought down the entire banking industry. The causes for the housing crisis are complicated, and while I do not want to rehash the whole story here, I do suggest reading *The Big Short* by Michael Lewis or watching the movie version directed by Adam McKay if you want to learn the details. The primary cause of the financial crisis was the deregulation of the banking industry. Without government intervention in bank activities, many banks were able to take riskier and riskier positions with speculative investments, often using margin ("margin" is a fancy way of saying loans). In other words, banks were using borrowed money to gamble with. As an example, imagine you borrowed $1,000 from a generous family member. Little do they know that you are going to take that $1,000 and place a bet with it. If the bet wins, you triple your money ($1,000 becomes $3,000). But if it loses, you owe the same amount ($1,000 becomes -$1,000). Now you owe the casino $1,000 and you still owe your family the $1,000 you borrowed. As you can imagine, betting with borrowed money magnifies both your winners and your losers. Many banks were taking these risky bets on something called mortgage-backed securities (MBS). Basically, they are an asset that is tied to packages of house loans by regular people like you and me. The banks receive interest payments each month on their MBSs as people pay their loans. The investor (banks in this example) who buys a mortgage-backed security is essentially lending money to home buyers. The banks would base how much they paid for these bundles based on the quality of loans. The quality is inferred based on the homeowner's credit history, income, employment, etc. Lower quality means the mortgage owner is more likely to default, and therefore a "riskier" investment. Generally, they wanted to purchase mortgage loans in these bundles of exceedingly high quality. High-quality loans in theory should only be given to people with exceptional credit histories and large stable incomes. But unfortunately, the lending industry was giving mortgages to just about anybody, even if they had no business purchasing a lavish home. There is a funny scene from *The Big Short* movie, where Steve Carell's character is chatting with a stripper that says she has mortgages on five houses and a condo. The point of that scene was just to underscore how easy it was to get a mortgage, and how many people were taking out multiple mortgages they were unlikely to be able to afford over the long run. To make matters worse, the credit agencies that evaluate the "quality" of the loans completely dropped the ball, and people who could barely pay their mortgage each month were still sold as "prime," or extremely low risk. As time went on, more and more people started defaulting their loans, and when interest rates started to rise, there was a runaway effect where millions of people simply could not make their payments. In a span of weeks to months, the MBSs that banks were holding became worth a fraction of their initial price. Trillions of dollars were lost, major banks went out of business or needed government bailouts to survive, and millions of ordinary Americans lost their houses.

The banking and financial sectors deserved the scorn that was heaped onto them after the financial crisis. They took far too much risk, did not police themselves, and essentially behaved like gamblers giving into their greedy desires. But there is plenty of blame to go around. I want to conclude this month by pointing out that many people simply took loans for houses that were too large and expensive for their income. They also gave in to their greed, and they paid the price. When purchasing a new home, it is important that you take some personal responsibility and assess "Do I really need such a large house?" Just because you *can* take out a loan for $400,000 does not mean that you *should*. If you are unsure how much is too much, consider following the 28% rule. According to this rule, a household should not spend more than 28% of its total monthly income on housing costs, including the mortgage, insurance, HOA fees, and other costs. With a dash of personal responsibility, some savvy negotiation skills, and good timing, you will be well on your way to making a great home purchase, another major money milestone.

Chapter 7

July:
Vacation season . . . within reason

I spend a lot of time discussing my financial planning client's long-term goals, dreams, and wishes for the future. As part of the planning process, it is important to "dig deep" and think critically about what you want out of life, and the path to achieve it. I have spoken with thousands of people about their personal finances, and I can state pretty confidently that most people are pretty similar. They want enough money to retire relatively young, become financially independent, have a nice house, and travel. Vacation is perhaps the second most requested goal (besides retirement) for most Americans. The freedom to travel is something most people associate with happiness, security, and the type of adventurous lifestyle they aspire to have. According to Gallup polls, over half of Americans vacation each summer, usually for a week or less, though upwards of 15% will take more than two weeks.[18] July is the most popular month for both vacations and travel, likely because many families are beholden to the nine-month school schedule.

When I first began outlining my thoughts for July, my mind quickly defaulted to an elaborate mishmash of tips and advice on how to save money when you travel. But the more I thought about the role that travel takes in our lives, the more I began to realize there is something deeper, more intrinsic to our psyche about the need to travel. How much time do you spend each week daydreaming about being somewhere else? Hiking in the mountains? Lying on a beach, sipping a fancy cocktail? Camping with friends? Exploring the culture of a new city? Do you ever have the overwhelming desire to hop in a van, point it in any direction, and leave all your worldly possessions behind? Just drive off into the sunset and never worry again about endless e-mails or going to business meetings? I do. I think it is healthy to fantasize about escaping regular life. When people are on vacation, they can temporarily escape the pressures of their work life and focus on "living in the moment." When you can live in the moment, the creeping dread of "What am I forgetting?" or "How am I going to pay this bill next month?" is gone. You just exist. You can enjoy the people and places around you, without worrying about the next project or problem in your life. I think this is central to what people desire when they declare "financial independence and travel" as a major life goal.

The benefits of vacation can be astounding. Many studies have shown that taking time away from the job can have physical and psychological health benefits. People who take vacations have less stress, lower risk of heart disease, a better sense of well-being, and more motivation to achieve goals. According to the Gallup "well-being index," frequent travelers have much higher scores than those that travel less often.[19] Unfortunately, there is an epidemic of vacation deprivation in the United States. The deprivation is primarily for two reasons: lack of vacation time and not using vacation time that was already earned. A recent vacation usage study conducted for Expedia questioned 11,144 employed adults from 19 countries about work-life balance. Respondents from the United States, Japan, and Thailand reported the lowest vacation usage, with only ten days being used in 2018. Countries where citizens reported taking the highest average number of vacation days were Brazil, France, Germany, and Spain, with an average of about 30 vacation days used.[20] In comparison to other countries, Americans received less vacation time than many others in the survey. However, that is not the complete story because Americans received 14 days on average but only took 10. The U.S. does not have mandated paid leave by the government like many other countries, so usage tends to be filtered through your employer. While cost was considered the largest barrier to taking a vacation, 23% of U.S. workers said they were not taking a vacation because they wanted to bank vacation days, 17% said it was because they could not get time off work, and 13% reported feeling guilty when they took time off. In other words, 30% of Americans are either kept from using their vacation time or feel shame for doing so. Consequently, Americans view travel and vacation as something they do *after* their work life is over (i.e., in retirement). But given the health and psychological benefits, Americans should be going on vacation more often. A study released last year by the American Psychological Association concluded that vacations reduce stress by removing people from the activities and environments they associate with anxiety. The positive effects were usually short lived but sometimes lasted well after the vacation was over.[21] Restlessness and disrupted sleep are often associated with stress, so the psychological benefits of vacation are linked to better sleep patterns, lower depression, and overall higher quality of life. But the effects are not just psychological. A host of studies have highlighted the cardiovascular benefits of taking a vacation.[22] A National Institute of Health trial followed 12,000 men with high risks for coronary heart disease over nine years and found that men who take frequent annual vacations were 21% less likely to die for any reason and 32% less likely to die from heart disease. The largest and longest running study of cardiovascular disease (Framingham Heart Study) found that women who vacation rarely (once every six years or less) were almost eight times more likely to develop coronary heart disease compared to women who vacationed at least twice a year.

I hope you have noticed the clear point I am not so subtly trying to communicate. Vacations are good. They help limit stress and keep you healthy. Americans are bad at taking vacations and often feel pressure to ignore their hard-earned vacation time. Sadly, people view vacation and travel as a post-retirement goal when it is something that should be common during their prime working years. If vacationing is going to be part of your regular financial life, it becomes a major expense that needs to be planned for. There are three keys to a financially successful vacation: flexibility, budgeting, and advanced planning.

Most of us have a vision in our head of what our ideal vacation looks like. We know what hotel or resort we are staying at, what restaurants we want to try, and what our daily adventures look like. But that same vision that makes our trip exciting can strain our budget. It is quite easy to become stuck on an agenda and miss out on opportunities to remain flexible and save money. For example, flights during the off-season or on a weekday are often cheaper. Flexibility with your travel dates and arrival times can go a long way towards keeping travel expenses low. Similarly, flexibility in your accommodations can keep costs down. If you insist on staying at only one hotel or resort during peak travel times, you are going to pay much more. The good news is that you can plan your flexibility ahead of time. If you remain opportunistic as you develop your plan, you will have more time to research cheaper options and book cheaper flights. If your trip is only three weeks away, it is not possible to be opportunistic about booking. You can only take what you get. So, flexibility is important prior to the trip but also important *during* the tip. For example, imagine you booked a winery tour in advance from a local travel company. But when you arrived, you saw other vendors offering the same tour for half the price on a different evening. If your agenda has some flexibility, you can go for the cheaper option and adjust on the fly. Another good piece of advice is to travel and eat like the locals do. If you only talk to people within the tourism "bubble" like hotel and restaurant employees, they are likely to direct you to the more expensive places designed for tourists. In contrast, if you chat with the locals about where they prefer to eat, you are likely to find good food at a better price.

The second key is advance planning. This might seem to contradict my previous advice to stay flexible. How can you plan everything in advance while also staying flexible? Advanced planning in this context really means "don't wait till the last minute." My wife and I usually spend our vacations hiking the national parks across the U.S. and Canada. My wife is our designated vacation planner, and she tends to book a lot of our arrangements almost a full year ahead. Why do this? It really comes down to cost. If you travel during peak times, accommodations tend to run limited in supply, which drives the prices up. Alternatively, booking a full year in advance when the supply is higher will tend to lead to substantial savings, as much as 40% on lodging costs. I understand this is not feasible for everybody, but there is a significant financial benefit to booking in advance and prepaying. The same logic applies to any other service or event that becomes limited in supply. Plan your travel and vacation when the supply is high, and the demand is low. There can be impending disasters if you do not plan properly, so keep detailed records of all your travel correspondence. In 2017, blogger Deborah Rogers from The Gifted Rat was looking forward to a family Royal Caribbean Cruise to Cuba.[23] She thought she had meticulously planned for the trip and had all the documents her family needed. Rogers flew to Miami with her family and showed up at the port, ready to relax poolside with cocktails. To her horror, she discovered she did not receive an important notice from Royal Caribbean, stating that her children also needed passports for the cruise. She did not have those passports, and this meant her family not only missed the cruise but lost $2,152 in nonrefundable tickets.

There are some other financial perks of really doing your due diligence and researching your trip in advance. Currency exchange rates and geography are often ignored when considering a location. But if you take your vacation in a country with a favorable exchange rate compared to the American dollar, you can likely do more for less. For example, destinations like Guatemala, Nicaragua, and Mexico often have low overall costs and favorable exchange rates compared to the dollar. This bonus might mean better accommodations, eating out more frequently, and faster and more convenient travel. Hiring a private driver in Mexico is cheaper than renting in more expensive countries. So, you really need to think hard about geography. Do you want to experience the culture of Southeast Asia? Consider that most of the other countries in that region are about one-third of the cost of visiting Japan. Planning a trip to Norway or Switzerland? If you choose the Balkans or eastern Europe instead, your overall travel costs might be one-quarter the overall cost. For many trips, the destination might be nonnegotiable, and I understand that. But if it isn't, choosing the right destination and paying attention to currency exchange rates can save you some serious cash and just might lead to a better experience.

The final piece of our travel plan is to keep and maintain a budget. This is particularly true when traveling in an area where it is obvious that you are a tourist. You might not be able to tell, but in many areas, there might as well be a glowing red "sucker" sign above your head when it comes to the local tourism industry. They know you are on vacation and have your financial guard down, and they want to exploit it. Shortly after we married, my wife and I went on a Caribbean cruise that included Jamaica as one of the stops. In one of our excursions, we visited a small waterfall and creek, led by some locals that dropped us off a couple of miles from the cruise ship. We were shocked to find they were aggressively asking for $20 tips, just for dropping us off at the waterfall. Most people just went ahead and tipped them without thinking "Is this a normal amount to tip?" for what was essentially a three-minute drive to a waterfall. Most of the locals were able to take advantage of the tourist's willingness to spend. In their home country, most people would not be willing to tip $20 on top of the excursion cost, but we let our guard down on vacation. On that same trip, a man placed a little trinket in my wife's hands, and then abruptly declared that she owed him money. Many people might be intimidated in that situation and just pay the $5 for the trinket, but this man did not realize how cheap my wife was. She put it back in his hand and said, "No, thanks." Even though many of these tourist traps are obvious, many travelers end up overpaying, because "we are on vacation" or "you only live once" and that is justification for incurring expenses they might ordinarily scoff at. The tourism industry really is built around creating a false sense of urgency. Many people think they are not going to make it back to a destination for a long time, so they feel pressured to spend on items they can't get anywhere else. The reality is that in the internet age, you can pretty much get anything online, and most of the items that people purchase to commemorate their trip are cheap and mass-produced anyway.

Now that you know not to fall into the tourist traps, how do you stick to a budget? This part is trickier, because for many people, spending more = more vacation fun. I do not want to be the one to suggest limiting fun on vacation, but I do think you should have a specified daily goal in mind. Then you get to choose your battles each day and really optimize your spending. If you do not have a daily budget in mind, costs are going to quickly escalate because there is no "anchor" to keep you grounded. Many people get into trouble because they do a lot of "special occasion" spending they might ordinarily not. For example, perhaps you reserve cocktails and dessert to special occasion dinners like anniversaries, birthdays, or other celebrations. On vacation, many people might make cocktails and dessert the default. Those costs will add up quickly and destroy your budget. Also, consider how you spend at airports. On a business trip or during routine travel, you might bring a few snacks for the plane ride. But on vacation, anticipation is running high and you might go to some of the (ridiculously overpriced) airport restaurants and bars. Everyone knows they have massively inflated prices, but do not let the context of your travel (leisure vs work) determine whether you fall into these traps.

Hopefully if you plan on a vacation this July, these tips can help keep you from financial regret after the vacation is over. But if we have established anything this chapter, I hope it is the realization that vacations and travel are extremely beneficial and deserve to be a part of your financial plan as early as possible. Do not make the mistake of keeping travel as a retirement-only goal. With some planning and frugality, you can make going on adventures a regular part of your life.

Chapter 8

August:
Turn up the heat on your investments

I was incredibly lucky to spend eight fantastic years as a university professor, where I was able to foster my interests in math, science, and finance and prepare young minds for their exciting new careers. But shortly after I started my professorship, a series of events led me towards the path of financial planning and investment management, and until now, I have only hinted at the story. I think it is an interesting way to start August because my story really demonstrates how small mistakes in your investment decisions can lead to massive differences later in life. I started my career as a physical geoscientist, primarily preparing students for careers in the energy industry. Finance and geoscience use many of the same statistics, modeling, and approaches to analyze their data, so my transition between fields was seamless, and I spent many years working in both fields. However, my decision to completely devote my life to financial planning had a specific catalyst because it really showed me how easily people can get ruined by their own investment choices if they are not paying attention.

Regardless of where you work, most positions follow a very predictable first day. Before you can start working, you must fill out paperwork, make decisions about your benefits, and likely sit through hours of poorly made training videos. Sometimes the decision in the benefits office can have massive consequences, and it is something that most people easily gloss over. My first day as a college professor was in the middle of August, shortly after I defended my dissertation. I hastily completed my benefits paperwork and decided to go along with the default, "recommended" investment option for the state of Texas, a teacher's pension. Pensions can be a wonderful choice for lifelong educators because they tend to provide a monthly benefit in retirement that depends on your years of service. At the time, I was young and knew I was not going to be staying in that position for life. A pension was the wrong choice for me, but I went along with the default option and that choice cost me some serious cash.

My alternative option at the time was to open a traditional 401(k), but this required special enrollment, and I was strongly encouraged to take the default option by the benefits office. There really were three considerations that made this a terrible choice for me. First, your money in a pension fund sits as "cash" in a money market account and generally earns between 1% and 2% per year in interest. During the same eight-year interval, the S&P 500 index (a good proxy for the overall U.S. stock market) averaged gains of about 14% *per year*. Second, my university had a great employer match: employee puts in 6.5%, gets 6% of that matched in additional contributions. However, if you chose the pension option, your entire match goes into the public pension fund and not to you! In my situation, this translated into $350 per month I would have gotten in my 401(k) but not in a pension. Finally, my decision to enter the pension system was unable to be rescinded. After the initial enrollment period, your choice for retirement plan was locked in. I realized my mistake relatively quickly, but once the process started, it was impossible to switch out of the pension and into a 401(k).

What exactly did I miss out on by going with the default investment option at my university? The number is not easy to quantify, but let's give it a try. I would have been getting $380 per month (regular contribution) + $350 per month (matched contribution), compounded over eight years with an average return of around 14%, assuming I invested aggressively. Instead, I received $380 per month with an average return of around 1.5%, and a guaranteed eight-year service pension of around $1,073 per month in retirement. On the surface, it does not sound like that bad of a deal. If I end up living until the age of 90, I might be able to collect that pension for 30 years, right? While that is true, there is one important missing component in our comparison. Time before retirement. I was only 30 when I made this decision, which means I had 35 years of average market returns in my 401(k) to grow that money. Ultimately, the problem was that the pension option was wrong for *me*, not that it was a poor choice in general. I knew that I was not going to be in the pension system long enough to build a large service credit, and I had decades to allow the market to take advantage of my employer match and help it grow. In the end, I was able to pull out of the pension and reinvest that money after eight years. Without getting into the weeds on the details of the math, my "loss" for my poor decision was roughly around $45,000. That is a steep price to pay for my ignorance at the time.

When I discovered my mistake, it set a fire inside me to dig further into financial planning and investment management. I spent hours every day reading, writing, and thinking about finance and how to help people make better choices. I knew I had a problem when I accidentally stayed up to 4:00 am, reading about the intricacies of the Chinese stock market when I had to get up at 6:00 am to prepare to lecture. In my early 30s, with just a couple of years under my belt as a professor, I went back to school, got my certifications, took financial planning courses, and opened my firm. It was a gradual process, but I finally realized that this was the role I was supposed to play in life. Now that I've been involved in the field for years and I've spoken to thousands of people about their financial situation, it has affirmed my decision that most people could use some help, just like I did a decade ago. I've spoken to many folks that have made similar decisions with their 401(k), made poor fund or stock choices, or simply did not invest because they were afraid. This is one of the reasons I think most people should work with a financial planner. There are so many small nuances and choices that can have major ramifications for your life in the future. Having a partner to help along the way keeps you accountable and makes sure you can dodge the pitfalls that many people fall into.

One of the easiest concepts in all of finance to understand is "simple interest." When you make a payment on a loan with simple interest, the payment will initially go towards paying off that month's interest and then the remainder towards the principal value of the loan. Assuming you pay each month in full, the interest never accrues. Compound interest is slightly different, as it adds some of the monthly interest back onto the loan. That means in each successive month, you are paying new interest on old interest. Simple interest loans tend to be fairly consumer-friendly, particularly for people that pay their loan payments in full each month. Compound interest loans add interest back onto the principal value of the loan and can quickly grow and lead to a "runaway" effect that makes paying them down extremely difficult. In my experience, most people have no problem grasping the difference between simple and compound loan interest. However, they are often unable to make the leap in understanding in the opposite direction. That is, compound interest has massive benefits to your investments over time, particularly if your dividends and interest are being reinvested to buy additional shares, and you are receiving a free match through your employer retirement plan like a 401(k).

Financial planners and savvy investors are often fond of lecturing other people about the importance of starting to save for retirement as soon as possible. Many people in their twenties understandably struggle with considering their retirement plans because they are just starting out their careers and families. Retirement seems like an eternity away when you are 24, but as most of us folks in the workforce understand, the years start to fly by when you are out of college. There is a reason why the advice to start young is so commonplace. It turns out that time is the most critical component of utilizing compound interest to your advantage. This is because compound interest leads to an exponential growth of the size of your investment account. If you have waited until your 50s to start saving, you'll never benefit from the same type of exponential growth of somebody that started in their 20s or 30s. This is even more important if you are receiving free money from an employer match program, which allows for even greater growth and compounding of your investments.

Consider the following three people that invest identically, but take vastly different approaches in *when* they start saving for retirement:

- Emily starts saving $400 per month at the age of 25.

- Jason waits ten additional years and starts saving $500 per month at 35.

- Kelly waits even longer than Jason and starts saving at 40, but to try to catch up, puts $800 into her account each month.

Before we continue, consider who you think ends up with more money at age 65? Emily has a ten-year head start on Jason but saves

$100 less per month for her entire working life. Kelly waited until 40 but saves twice as much as Emily ($800 per month) for the next 25 years.

At first glance, it seems intuitive that Kelly should have the most money for retirement. After all, she contributed double the amount of Emily and contributed for 62.5% of the amount of time (25 vs 40 years). Our intuition says that her contribution of 100% of the amount of cash should more than make up for the 37.5% drop in time. But that is not true. Here are the actual results, assuming they all invested aggressively and got an 8% annual return:

- Emily 8% annual; 400/month for 480 months = $192,000 principal, $1,104,722 interest, $1,296,722 total.

- Jason 8% annual; 500/month for 360 months = $180,000 principal, $528,807 interest, $708,807 total.

- Kelly 8% annual; 800/month for 300 months = $240,000 principal, $491,872 interest, $731,872 total.

As you can see, the power of compounding means your total account value does not linearly correlate with how much you placed into the account. In other words, Jason only waited 25% longer (ten years out of 40 in the workforce) before contributing to his retirement account, but he ended up with only 55% of Emily's total at retirement. Time is your most important ally in generating wealth for a comfortable retirement. Kelly invested aggressively and saved much more than either Jason or Emily, but she was unable to even come close to Emily, who will be much better off in her golden years.

I hope now the concept of time is firmly entrenched in your mind as the key to your investing success. The next piece of the puzzle is *timing*, which while similar, opens a whole other can of worms. I have found this to be one of the most common mistakes that amateur investors make. In fact, mistakes made trying to time the market are so deeply held by most people, that a financial planner can earn their fee 10x over just by keeping people from buying and selling at the worst possible moments. There is a common adage in the finance industry that goes "time in the market beats timing the market." This is unequivocally true. Nobody knows exactly when the market is going to drop or when it is going to rise, and trying to pick the tops and bottoms is fruitless at best. It is like trying to catch a bullet with a pair of chopsticks. Maybe you'll get it, but probably not. So, the next logical question is: *When* do I invest? The answer is *right now*. You can't time the market, so the earlier the better, as we learned from our example with Emily, Jason, and Kelly. Many people are terrified of investing and accidentally buying in at the height of the market. Instead, they think "we should wait until the market dips." I know people that have been waiting for the market to dip since 2009. Maybe they eventually bought back into the market during the coronavirus drop in March 2020. But guess what? Even if they called the bottom of the market in March, they would have been much better off investing back in 2009. Or 2010, 2011, 2012, 2013, 2014, or 2015. Literally at any point over the past decade would have been better, and they would have doubled or even tripled their money. The reality is that the stock market is almost always near its all-time high. The only exception would be during a major recession, or in a smaller correction (about a 10% loss) that tends to happen once or twice every year. If you could predict which day out of the entire year would be the lowest, you would be the greatest investor who has ever lived. But you can't, so it is best to just stay invested the whole time.

It is true that the market is going to go down. It might even crash the day after you invested your money. But it is still always the right move to invest as soon as you are able. Nobody can tell you exactly when the next market correction or crash is going to happen. The best investors in the world can't tell you, JP Morgan can't tell you, that guy on YouTube can't tell you, and your Bitcoin obsessed co-worker *definitely* can't tell you. It will happen at some point, but anyone that tells you they know when it is going to happen is speculating or just outright lying. The talking heads on financial media sowed massive panic during the market drop in March 2020. Many people understandably pulled all their money from the stock market and held cash, waiting for the world to return to normal before investing again. Those people lost out on the massive market recovery that took place from March until the end of the year. The best choice you could have made was to do nothing. If it just so happens that you are unlucky and the market crashes shortly after you invested, *you still made the right choice.* It might be tough to watch your assets plummet in value but consider what is really happening behind the scenes. The whole time your assets are moving down in value, you are accumulating dividends and interest that are getting reinvested back into your account. Those dividends and interest purchase additional shares, so when the market eventually moves back up, you own more shares than if you had waited until the crisis was over. So not only is there a huge opportunity cost lost for trying to time the market and being wrong, functionally you accumulate more shares, and it is still the right move to invest as early as possible.

One of the most internet famous examples of market timing was developed by Ben Carlson of Ritholtz Wealth Management in 2014. He made a blog post that introduced Bob, the world's worst hypothetical investor.[24] Bob just so happened to invest at the peak of the market, at the absolute worst time throughout his entire life. But Bob never wavered and consistently invested his earnings for decades, always at the worst moment each year. He focused on building wealth over time, and always had the worst timing. Even with his bad luck, while only investing between $2,000–$8,000 per year, he ended up a millionaire with $1,100,000 saved for retirement. Time in the market triumphs timing the market yet again.

In 2018, I had a relatively long meeting with a prospective financial planning client. Let's call her "Melissa" for the purpose of this example. Melissa told me a story that I've unfortunately heard many times over the years, but nonetheless, never ceases to shock me. She was near retirement, single, and had worked diligently her whole career in the manufacturing industry. She paid little attention to an old 401(k) that was rolled over into an IRA nearly ten years ago. But finally, in 2018, after hearing her co-workers gush about their investment performance, Melissa took a closer look. Her investments were barely earning any interest at all and had not earned more than 1% or 2% for almost ten years. She booked an appointment with me to discuss what she could be doing differently. The bad news was that the default investment setting in Melissa's IRA was just a generic money market sweep. In other words, she had not owned any actual stock funds for nearly ten years and had never really invested her funds! She assumed that the IRA account was automatically investing for her, and this is a grave error that I see many people make when they are first starting out learning about their investments.

The fundamental mistake that Melissa made was misunderstanding the difference between "baskets" (401(k), 403(b), IRA, 529, brokerage accounts) and the things inside the basket (stocks, bonds, mutual funds, ETFs). For people that are financially savvy, this is an obvious distinction, but I've seen the mistake enough over the years to know the confusion is commonplace. Baskets are types of accounts. They have different limits on how much a person can add to them, when they can add to them, and how they are taxed when they eventually start pulling items out of the basket. In other words, the baskets all have different shapes, sizes, and rules on what they can hold and when the items can be pulled out. In contrast, the items inside the basket are your actual investments, and they need to be purchased by a broker that allows both amateurs and professionals to access public markets. If you never put any items in your basket, you will be left holding cash. The most common basket item is stock shares of public companies, which represent a tiny sliver of ownership in that company. Bonds are another basket item, which are essentially money that you loan a company or government and then they pay you a monthly amount before eventually giving you back your principal after a specified amount of time. Bonds are heavily tied to interest rates, so they tend to be much lower risk, lower reward compared to stock. Other basket items include real estate investment trusts (REITS), commodities like gold, oil, copper, or grain, and even cryptocurrencies (though these are still not easily available in retirement plans).

The most important basket item for most people is *funds*. Funds can own all the items we just discussed, but instead they own them in large quantities to decrease risk. For example, you could purchase shares in just Amazon, Facebook, or Tesla on their own. Alternatively, you could buy an S&P 500 index fund, which owns shares of 500 of the largest American companies and weighs them based on their size. Individual company stock moves up and down drastically from day to day, but funds tend to be more stable because they represent an average of a much larger pool of companies. These swings are called *volatility*, and it is an important concept in investing. Bonds can also be owned in funds, and those also tend to be much lower risk than owning an individual bond. Consider the following scenario: You loan a large software company $10,000, and in return they agree to pay you 4% on your $10,000 for the next five years, before eventually returning your principal at the end of the fifth year. What happens if their company is rocked by scandal, runs into major financial problems, or loses a huge amount of market share to a competitor? If they go bankrupt, they might default on your bond, making it more difficult for them to pay what they owe. Even if you see the writing on the wall, it might be difficult to find a buyer for your bonds, since nobody is going to want to take on the risk for a company that is struggling. This concept is called *liquidity*, which is essentially how easy an asset is to buy and sell in a market. Individual bonds are not very liquid, which makes them hard to buy and sell, especially if a company is struggling financially. Bond funds, however, are groups of hundreds of bonds for a variety of different companies or governments. If one or two of those companies go bankrupt, your exposure to risk is still minimized. They are also more liquid, so you can dispose of them when you need to.

I've mentioned several times that I think most people should work with financial planners to develop their investment portfolios. Their knowledge on different sectors, fund costs, rebalancing, and tax optimization can really save most people serious money in the long run. However, if you want to implement an investment and savings plan for yourself, I have three general suggestions:

1. Understand your baskets.

2. Diversify the assets in your baskets.

3. Place the assets in your baskets in the right order.

Understanding the nuances of the variety of investment baskets can be daunting. The acronyms alone are enough to drive most people mad: 403(b), 401(k), 457, 529, HSA, FSA, IRA, ROTH, SEP, SIMPLE. If you really hate yourself, you can try and learn the differences between types of trusts: marital, bypass, living, AB, ABC, revocable, irrevocable, testamentary, charitable, credit shelter, and so on. Clearly, exploring these different baskets is well beyond the scope of

Money Milestones. But there are some key points to remember. First, IRAs (Individual Retirement Accounts) and your employer-sponsored plans are usually tax deductible, depending on your household income. Interest and dividends inside the accounts accumulate tax-sheltered until you withdraw money from them, usually after at the age of 59.5. This allows you to defer paying taxes on your income and earnings until later in your life. You might also have a ROTH IRA or 401(k), which is not tax deductible, but can be withdrawn tax-free in retirement. All the accounts above have contribution limits (how much you can add each year), different tax treatment, income limits (your income determines if you can contribute and how much), and different rules for withdrawals and penalties. You need to understand these baskets before you start using them.

You also want to diversify the items inside your baskets. Nobody wants to go on a picnic with only plain bread in the basket. You need to add some meat and cheese, vegetables, and dessert. Your picnic (and your retirement) will be more successful. This means you should diversify between what we call asset classes: U.S. stock, international stock, large companies (large cap), medium and small companies, emerging markets, government and corporate bonds, and even alternatives like real estate, gold, or cryptocurrencies. The key to diversification is that you have some assets that are not correlated with each other. Bonds might go down one month, while U.S. stock soars. Or perhaps foreign emerging markets like China have a great year, while the U.S. market suffers. Diversification decreases risk and lends your portfolio some stability against risks associated with specific governments, companies, or even political unrest. Secondly, your portfolio needs to be diversified by sector. Sectors include technology, communication services, consumer, energy, financial services, healthcare, and more. Your portfolio should be exposed to many different types of industries to protect your money against sector underperformance. In March 2020, tensions between Russia and Saudi Arabia in combination with the lack of travel from COVID-19 lockdowns devastated the oil industry and the stock of most energy companies. If you held mostly energy stocks in 2020, you had a real bad year. But the technology and healthcare sectors did great, and if you were appropriately diversified, you would have had no problem balancing out the disruption in the oil sector.

Finally, you want to put your investments inside your baskets in the right order. The "right order" depends on your personal situation, but there are some basic guidelines that work for most people. You always want to take advantage of free money before any other consideration. That means if your employer includes a company match, always contribute at least that amount before considering any other baskets. Why would you ever not take free money? Obviously, if it is a question of feeding your family and contributing 5% to your 401(k), you would not take the free money, but if the option is there, you should take it. After hitting your employer match, you then want to switch gears and max your IRA. In 2020, people under 50 can contribute $6,000 and folks over can contribute $7,000. IRAs generally provide you with more options than employer plans for lower fees. If you still have more money left, you want to go back and max your 401(k) or equivalent. If you still have more available money after maxing your IRA and employer plan then you want to investigate other tax-sheltered plans like Health Savings Accounts (HSAs) or 529s (College Savings Plans), but it really depends on your goals, and financial situation. If those plans are not available to you, or not necessary, then your excess funds should go into taxable baskets like brokerage accounts or living trusts. I see many people investing in taxable accounts before their IRA and retirement plans are maxed. If you are saving for retirement, this is a poor decision. Why would you pay taxes for decades if you did not have to? The only reason to use a taxable account before a tax-sheltered plan would be if you need the money relatively soon, though there are still options for using plans like ROTH IRAs, which allow you some flexibility for removing your funds prior to age 59.5. Opening and funding your first investment accounts is a critical money milestone and one that will reap massive rewards in the future.

Chapter 9

September:
Back to school: Invest in yourself

There is a palpable feeling of excitement surrounding the "back to school" season. Parents are eagerly shopping for new clothes and school supplies, and let's be honest, looking forward to getting their kids out of the house for a few hours each day. Teachers are building their curricula, networking, and starting their grand plans for the year. School-age students, while lamenting the end of the summer, are still looking forward to seeing their friends and getting some structure back to their lives. New college students are bright-eyed, optimistic, and looking forward to a new social life and the beginnings of a lifelong career. Like most annual traditions in the United States, the start of the school year is an excuse for retailers to begin new sales, drive traffic to their stores and websites, and create a spectacle to the buying public. For those far removed from the importance of the back-to-school season, it is easy to just see it as another capitalistic cash grab as opposed to the opportunities it can bring. September represents new beginnings, career change, and most importantly, the opportunity to *invest in yourself*. After all, you are your biggest investment in life. Nothing else in this book matters if you can't secure stable housing, an income, and put food on the table for your family. Part of that is developing a skill set, getting a job, and contributing to society (your financial Return on Investment, ROI). The other part is more intangible. You can invest in your emotional well-being, your mental health, social skills, and generally improve as a person (self-ROI). If you improve yourself, you will be a more desirable employee, friend, and partner, which means a better chance at securing the stable income and lifestyle that most people crave so deeply.

Like many people that have made the poor decision (just kidding . . . sort of) to spend 10+ years in college, I've spent some serious time hanging around college campuses. After I graduated with my degree, I went to work at a medium-size liberal arts university. Most universities in the U.S. are rooted in the liberal arts tradition, which stresses a broad knowledge base in philosophy, history, and social science. Traditionally, the idea was to help you become a more well-rounded, educated individual before you entered adulthood. The liberal arts tradition really stresses "knowledge for knowledge's sake" as opposed to a narrow skill set that one might develop at a trade school or other training program. Personally, I think there is a lot of value in the liberal arts tradition. We want our fellow Americans to be well informed and better critical thinkers, particularly when it comes to environmental, political, or social issues. If you have broad exposure to different worldviews and ideas, it is generally easier to converse with others and hold conversations about events impacting all of us. In other words, the self-ROI of a liberal arts degree is extremely high. But what about the financial ROI? In the past, getting a liberal arts education had massive financial *and* self-ROI because most people did not go to college. Just having a degree gave you a leg up on the hiring market. But over the past few decades, undergraduate degrees have become more common, and the needs of employers are more technical and specialized. This has changed the landscape somewhat, as a liberal arts background now gives more self-ROI than it does financial ROI. So, is it still worth it to get a traditional, broad-based four-year degree? With college costs rising at an astounding 4–8%[25] inflation rate, it only makes sense to question the viability of the financial ROI of an undergraduate degree.

Our first step is to evaluate just the averages. Maybe you do not consider yourself average, but someone must be, and it is a good way to evaluate the relative value of a college degree. The financial ROI of a college education has two main components: How much will you make and will you get a job? The former does not matter if you can't achieve the latter. On average, your weekly earnings are much higher with a degree to your name:

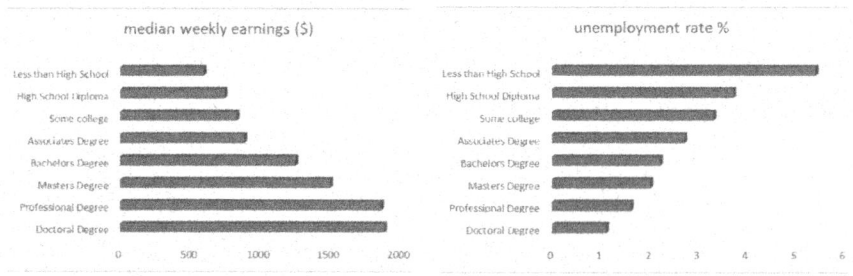

Data are for people aged 25 and over, working either for full-time wages or as salaried employees. Source: U.S. Bureau of Labor Statistics[26]

Clearly, *on average*, getting a degree helps with our first component of financial ROI, making more money. More specifically, this graph shows the median wage difference, which is the "middle" value in a list of numbers. The median is less influenced by large numbers, so the earnings are less effected by outliers, like a business owner that dropped out of high school but still makes an income of $500,000 a year. The median adult who holds a high school degree makes about

$747 per week compared to $1,248 for someone with a bachelor's degree. Master's and professional degrees also seem to pay off handsomely, with weekly wages of $1,497 and $1,861 respectively. The financial ROI of a high school degree is also pretty large, as those without a diploma only make around $592 per week. It would be hard for anyone to look at these numbers without concluding that education has a great benefit for your lifelong earning potential. But the more relevant question is: Is it worth it after paying for college? Again, if we just consider large-scale patterns, the average student has about $27,700 in loan debt if they graduated from a four-year public school, and $30,800 if the university was private.[27] Based on the average student loan interest rate of 4.66% over the past 15 years, and a 20-year term, the lifetime cost of a bachelor's degree is $42,636 for public and $47,407 for private school. That is a lot of money. However, it pales in comparison to the average increase of $501 per week, $2,004 per month, or $26,052 per year the person with a bachelor's degree makes over someone with just a high school diploma. Over a 40-year work history, that is over one million dollars difference! To further reinforce this trend is the difference in unemployment rate. There is a clear and gradual decline in unemployment rate with degree level. If you spend more time employed, you make more money. All the logic we just used on college degrees also applies to trade schools and more specialized training programs. Obviously, we can't go sector by sector, looking at different trades and training programs, but in general, more education and training leads to more income.

I've been tracking the debate about student loans and the viability of college degrees for nearly a decade. To my dismay, there has been a large movement recently to try and dissuade people from getting more education because of the increased costs of attending college. It is clearly a problem that education costs increase by 8% some years when inflation tends to hover around 2%. But as a society, we are still a very long way from being to a point where college degrees are worthless, and it's clear from the discussion above that education is a great investment for most people. But like many of the financial decisions we have discussed in *Money Milestones*, the details need to be evaluated before you commit to the decision. Earlier in the chapter, I mentioned how many fields in the liberal arts tradition had high self-ROI but declining financial ROI, at least compared to 20th century standards. This is where the choice really starts to matter because the devil is in the details. While our median weekly income and unemployment differ drastically by education level, they also strongly diverge by major. Newly employed graduates aged 25–29 in electrical engineering make about $78,700 per year with only a 1.9% unemployment rate.[28] Nurses in the same age demographic make $58,700 annually with only a 1.7% unemployment rate. Along with other types of engineering, finance, healthcare, IT, and business fields, these are high financial ROI degrees. In contrast, fine arts majors make about $40,500 after graduation but must tackle a 3.7% unemployment rate. Elementary education teachers also have median pay of about $40,500 but are more easily employed (1.3% unemployment). These are low financial ROI majors, along with history, psychology, literature, social work, and other types of humanities. Based on the student loan math we mentioned prior, it is certainly possible to get into a position where a long bout of unemployment followed by a low-paying job could make your education investment a raw deal. So, you need to decide your primary objective when trying to make an investment in yourself. Is this a financial decision for your future? Or are you trying to invest in your general knowledge, experience, and breadth as a person? If a degree in 17th century poetry can't get you a job, what does it get you? Is it possible to get a job just by having interesting things to talk about at a cocktail party? I would make the argument that investing in yourself in nonfinancial ways can open some doors for you, but likely only when combined with some actual training and a useful skill set.

Many of us are probably aware of the stereotype of the socially awkward person that can't get a date, has difficulty holding down a steady job, and generally just repels everyone around them. We live in a social society, and there are long-term consequences (financial and otherwise) for not being able to easily integrate and work well with others. The reality is that appearance, charm, wit, and likeability really play a role in getting hired for jobs, in addition to the more obvious rewards, like making friends and finding relationships. Many of us have probably seen people that were unqualified for a new position rise to the top of a company purely on the strength of their connections and relationships with others. Being connected can unfortunately completely outweigh credentials and experience in the workforce. The good news is that many of these skills can be learned, and I consider them the other side of the "invest in yourself" coin. Education and training give you a direct financial reward in your career. Being a likeable, confident, charismatic person can give you an indirect reward by opening up opportunities and allowing for easier advancement. For some people, this comes naturally, and others will need to make a greater time investment to improve themselves.

There are many different nonfinancial ways to invest in yourself. Many of these suggestions could be misconstrued as a personal attack if they were coming from a friend or family, so what better way to hear them than as typed words from a stranger? If a loved one tells you to "invest in yourself" or improve yourself physically, emotionally, and creatively, that is going to be an open invitation for an argument. But from a logical standpoint, it really does pay off in the long run to try and improve who you are as a partner, co-worker, or friend. Have you noticed the trend among people to get very bored with their careers after just a few years? People that were once driven and hungry, slowly getting replaced by shells of their former selves. This is because they have become complacent. I noticed this among university faculty that really got stuck into a monotonous routine and really lost their drive to do research, push the boundaries, and find ways to contribute to their fields. So, the first way to invest in yourself is by learning new skills. This could be the obvious training programs and certifications, or it could be something completely outside your wheelhouse. Learn a language, start programming, learn new types of software, write, teach workshops, start an online business, literally anything to keep you engaged. Later in your career, those new skills just might get you a new job, a networking opportunity, or help you reach your goals sooner. "Side hustles" are blowing up in popularity, and I have a hunch that it is not only because of the financial benefits but also the confidence and excitement of learning new things.

The social counterpart to "learning new things" is "associate with new people." Many of us tend to live in political, socio-economic, and career-based echo chambers. But if you associate with the types of people you might not ordinarily encounter in daily life, you will certainly gain new perspectives and develop your friend and business network. Again, you never know if one of these relationships will lead to a new career or opportunity. We can take this one step further as well and say, "Associate with good people." You can't succeed financially if you surround yourself by those that do not see the benefits of your efforts or discourage you from making positive change in your life, financial or otherwise. Changing your financial situation can be an enormous undertaking that requires some sacrifice, discipline, and consistency. If you surround yourself with friends and family that keep you account-able and celebrate your successes, it will provide the confidence you need to stick to your financial plan. In contrast are the "friends" or co-workers that try and sabotage your efforts. Telling you to buy that fancy new car that you know you can't afford or shaming you for not attending expensive dinners or vacations. These are the same people that shove donuts in your face every day when you are on a diet!

"Thank you for coming in to interview for a position with XYZ Bread Co. As you know, we have interviewed several candidates for this position. We regret to inform you that you have not been selected for this position. We wish you success in your ongoing career search." Sounds familiar? Even if you have done everything correctly, the perfect resume, excellent qualifications, and great letters of recommendation, you still might have trouble getting hired. Sometimes there was just a better candidate. But there could be something else at work if history keeps repeating itself, and you just can't get hired for the jobs you are qualified for. It might hurt to hear, but it could have been your personality. More importantly, it could have been how your personality was *perceived* by the interviewers. It is difficult for people to get a quick sense of who you are personally, and they might make snap judgements about your likeability and fit with the company. But there are some ways to improve yourself when it comes to perception. The last two types of personal investment really dictate how you see yourself in the world, and consequently how others see you. They are "personality investment" and "physical investment." This does not mean you might have a "bad personality," but it could mean that you need to invest and train yourself to show more of your personality, or work on physical factors (sleep, appearance, health) that will make you more confident and energetic to your peers.

In the workplace, your attitude and personality can make or break your financial future. Your ability to work and cooperate with other team members, customers, or clients is critical to maintaining steady employment, progressing in your career, and getting raises. But it is critical that you focus inward first, rather than trying to present yourself as something that you are not. In my experience, the inability to shift your mindset and understand alternative viewpoints is one of the major causes of friction in the workplace. An emotional or personality investment requires you to shift your mindset and see something through the lens of another. This can be about finding ways to help your brain focus and placing yourself in a more relaxed state of mind. An "investment" would be something like meditation, exercise, hiking, or even just calmly collecting the opinions of people around you that might have different viewpoints. It sounds obvious, but many people need to try to learn *how* to see the world from different perspectives and change their personality and attitude in response.

I've previously discussed my transition from an overweight teenager into a healthy adult, and the grit and self-motivation necessary to make that change. What I did not mention was another crucial component of that transition. The personality change that happens *as a result of* making a physical investment. A physical investment can be exercise, weight loss, getting better sleep, eating healthier, or a host of other things. But the primary beneficiary of those improvements is your increase in self-esteem and confidence. If you like yourself more, others will as well. And as we already established, if other people like you, that will translate into career and financial success. These patterns are not just nice words on a page either, there is hard data that shows improvements in job performance, self-esteem, and confidence with exercise. In a study done in Baltimore in 2016, employees that exercised, showed statistically significant improvements in job performance, mood, and subjective health.[29] Employees that exercised were more productive at work, felt healthier, and engaged with their co-workers in a more friendly manner ("mood" in the study). As a result of many of these types of studies, there has been an effort by business owners and corporations to encourage exercise and healthcare incentives for their employees. It is a win-win investment for everybody, since productivity, morale, and social interactions all improve at the business.

Shortly before I left graduate school, I had an interview with a major energy company for a research and project management position. I spent hours researching the company, the financials and science behind their projects, and how my experience and research would benefit their team. I was thinking about the interview via the lens of my experience as a "numbers guy." Guess what? My interview had no technical questions, and they seemed to not care at all about any of my experience and technical know-how. I was completely caught off guard. Instead, the interviewer asked only very poignant personality questions. I did not realize it at the time, but I was being given modified verbal questions from a Caliper or Myers-Briggs profile test. I was not prepared for it, and I did not get a callback for a second interview. These personality tests are often given online now, and some preparation can give you an opening to get a new career. Many studies have shown that employees placed into positions that do not match their personality often have lower engagement, which leads to lower productivity and higher turnover. Companies understandably do not want to train employees only for them to become unproductive and leave their position shortly after training. The take-home point is that certain personalities are better for certain positions, and you need to know what they are. You can "invest" in yourself by preparing for these exams but also trying to learn what traits correspond to your specific field or position and then making the effort to internalize those changes into your life. Obviously, you can "fake" the personality traits, but you would be much better served by trying to change your outlook in order to choose a career or position that is best suited to you personally. Ultimately, good fit = better career = more money.

In September, we have stumbled upon something crucial in our personal finance journey. Education and training lead to a direct financial return on investment (ROI), but self-improvement leads to "self-ROI," and that can influence our financial ROI. In other words, education and training is important to meet your career goals, and there is a direct relationship between your salary and unemployment if you do so. However, investing in your personal, physical, and social abilities can get you jobs, open doors, help you advance in your career, and ultimately make you the kind of person that others want to be around. That is just as important, if not more important to achieving your personal finance goals.

Chapter 10

October: How to avoid financial vampires
(Halloween edition)

Most of us who grew up in the 1980s and early 1990s have fond memories of roving across the neighborhood during Halloween, collecting our bounty of candy, and spending the evening with our friends or family. Things seemed a bit different back then. The world seemed like it was a little bit safer, parents were more willing to give their kids autonomy to collect candy from strangers, and the experience was magical for your average chocolate-loving preteen. For those of us who lived in the suburbs, our bikes were the perfect form of transportation, allowing us easy access to a nearly infinite number of houses to eagerly attack for free candy, with the rare "jackpot" of a normal-size Snickers bar being the highlight of the evening. Today, social media is littered with people complaining that trick-or-treating has declined over the last 20 years and is a shadow of its former self. Kids no longer stay out until midnight without parental supervision, certain areas have extremely low turnout and have turned into "candy deserts," and the overall vibe is now one of suspicion towards strangers, not fun with your neighbors. According to a report from the National Retail Federation's (NRF) annual Halloween survey, the number of Americans who say they're planning to take their kids trick-or-treating has been roughly 30% since 2005.[30] But the NRF includes all adults in their survey, including those without kids, so many of the respondents that do not participate might just be childless households. Other surveys, such as one conducted in 2011 by Safe Kids Worldwide, found that 73% of parents still take their kids trick-or-treating, casting doubt on the claims by many that trick-or-treating is dead.[31]

If trick-or-treating is not dead, why does it seem to so many that neighborhood streets are now devoid of happy children with their bags of candy on Halloween night? It is because the streets *are* missing the same number of children they used to have. There has been a fundamental shift in *where* people take their kids to celebrate Halloween. Since 2005, there has been a rapid rise in alternative trick-or-treating events hosted by businesses, community centers, and churches. Some are "trunk-or-treat" events, where parents decorate their cars, and community children walk from car to car, grabbing as much candy as they can. These types of community events are often cited for their safety and lack of "stranger danger," so they are more appealing to parents. While there is no doubt this is a concern for many parents, I'm not buying it as the primary driver of the evolutionary change of trick-or-treating. I think the real reason these events have taken over Halloween is simply because they are easier for parents. Instead of driving from neighborhood to neighborhood looking for good houses, or from the outskirts into the suburbs, parents can skip the hassle and just show up to one place. This is of particular importance for people who live in highly fragmented communities with separate city, suburban, and rural centers. Transportation is often a driver of societal change, and in this case, less driving is simply easier. Ease of access to affordable transportation is mandatory for many people to be able to maintain a certain type of lifestyle. And that is where our story turns back to personal finance. Just like the "old days" of trick-or-treating would be a drain on time and effort for parents, many vehicles are a drain on your finances. When our vehicle purchases move beyond "basic transportation" to status symbols, they turn into something downright horrifying. In the celebration of Halloween, we're going to call them "financial vampires." Scary.

I received my driver's license back in the dark ages of the mid-1990s. As a teenager, concerned with my status in the high school "coolness" hierarchy, obviously I needed a sweet ride to impress the ladies. But there was a problem with that. I had no money and neither did my parents. So, I ended up with a beige 1983 Oldsmobile Cutlass Ciera, falling apart, rusty, and barely running. Not exactly the epitome of "cool," more like a dorky rectangle of 1980's browns and yellows. I had a string of terrible, barely functioning "beaters" in the late 1990s and early 2000s but I was extremely lucky. My father was a mechanic and would fix my cars repeatedly, patching them with temporary fixes, junkyard parts, and just enough elbow grease to keep them going year after year. At the time, I was jealous of my classmates who often had expensive, newer cars. But looking back on it, I realize my dad taught me an incredibly important personal finance lesson. When you just need basic transportation, there is absolutely no reason to waste money on a vehicle other than what your lifestyle can afford. Anything above that is purely for "status." And status is a waste of money for the fiscally responsible.

I define a financial vampire as an asset whose value rapidly depreciates shortly after purchase and continues to decline in value as time goes on. Common examples are vehicles, boats, expensive jewelry, and other luxury items. Have you ever heard the joke that a boat is a hole in the water that you throw money into? It is a perfect example of a financial vampire. The moment you walk away from the dealership or store, you have already lost a huge amount of money that you can't recover. In addition, expensive cars and trucks cost more to insure and repair, which compounds the financial losses even further. There are many examples of items where "you get what you pay for." Surely it makes sense that higher quality materials mean better construction, better attention to detail, and a product that is more reliable and has a longer useful lifetime. But the car industry has not really evolved that way. In fact, the most reliable, longest lasting, and lowest maintenance costs cars tend to be the cheaper ones! More expensive cars and trucks tend to focus more on optional amenities, detailing, power, and of course, status.

So, what is the price of that status upgrade over the long run, and how does it impact our larger investment and retirement goals? A 2017 auto reliability survey conducted by Consumer Reports asked subscribers to assess their annual maintenance and repair costs over a ten-year period by the make of the car.[32] While luxury car manufacturers (BMW, for example) would often have free maintenance costs for the first few years, the costs would skyrocket over the lifetime of the car. In the end, ten-year (2007–2017) maintenance and repair costs for "luxury" manufacturers like Audi, BMW, Jaguar, and Volvo were often over $1,000 per year, while lower cost manufacturers like Toyota, Ford, and Hyundai would hover near $400 per year. While $600 per year does not sound like an incredible amount of money, keep in mind that these costs are in addition to the massive initial price difference and subsequently your monthly loan payment. Let's consider a simple example:

Car 1: 2019 Volvo S60 (new, $41,295 msrp), ten-year upkeep $10,000

Car 2: 2019 Hyundai Sonata (new, $22,500 msrp), ten-year upkeep $4,000

At first glance, you might say the ten-year difference in price is $18,795 + $6,000 = $24,795. A significant amount of money but perhaps not crippling to somebody with a decent salary and stable job. But there is an additional *opportunity cost* loss here as well. As we have mentioned priorly, opportunity cost represents the benefit that is missed out on when one alternative is taken with money at the expense of another. In "August" (chapter eight), we talked about the power of compound interest. In this example, the opportunity cost of a more upscale vehicle is remarkably high because we lost the opportunity to invest that money into our IRA, 401(k), or brokerage account, where it would compound our return. Let's just assume we paid cash for both Hyundai and Volvo in year one and then paid our annual upkeep costs for the next ten years. If that $18,795 is invested immediately, and then we invest our upkeep savings of $500 each year, the ten-year value of that money is $44,364.41 (assuming "average" stock returns of 7% per year). Staggeringly, the 20-year value of that money is $94,663.31. That is the true cost of picking a more expensive "status" symbol for your vehicle. Now throw in a second car, a boat or camper, and a few more financial vampires into the mix over 20 years and you can quickly see how these costs can seriously inhibit your ability to retire when you want.

It is one thing to point out that vehicles are financial vampires, but of course, a good financial planner still needs to discuss a "plan" with their clients on how to approach buying their next car. After all, the average American commutes nearly 30 minutes to work each day, and according to the U.S. Census Bureau, those times are increasing over time. Obviously, we need cars to get to work, to take little Jimmy to soccer practice, and to have the freedom to travel in a way that affords us the lifestyle we are accustomed to. But do we need brand-new cars? From a personal finance standpoint, the answer is unequivocally *no*. Most online "car affordability calculators" suggest that the average person should keep their car loan payment at or below ten percent of their gross (pre-tax) monthly income. Using those guidelines, a family which earns $75,000 per year can afford a monthly car payment of $625. While I agree that $625 is affordable for a family that brings home $75,000 per year, it is certainly not optimal, and in my opinion a waste of money. As we noted above, paying high vehicle costs can siphon away your available cash and subsequently your ability to retire early. So, the answer is to account for retirement savings or net worth when considering your car payment. A sliding scale allows wealthier people to "splurge" on more expensive vehicles without impacting their overall progression towards a solid retirement. I suggest that the average family limit their car payment to 5% of their monthly gross income or less, with a provision to increase that by 1% for every $100,000 they have in net worth (assets minus liabilities, as we discussed earlier). The easiest way to do this is to only purchase used cars. According to carfax.com, most cars lose more than 10% of their value during the first month after you drive them off the lot. That is essentially a 10% surcharge for purchasing a new car, with no added benefit other than the novelty of being the only owner. You might as well just light cash on fire! According to current vehicle depreciation rates, the value of a new vehicle will drop by more than 20% within the first year of ownership, then about 10% annually thereafter. Owing $20,000 on a vehicle with a Kelley Blue Book value of only $10,000 is an uncomfortable position that I see many of my clients in. Vehicles tend to depreciate faster than you can pay them off, and they are aptly named financial vampires because they literally "suck" away your free cash into a black hole of lost value.

Cars and trucks are the most common financial vampires that most people tend to purchase, but there are worse ones, such as RVs, boats, and expensive jewelry. The history of diamond rings is rife with intrigue, shady business deals, and manipulative marketing. The international corporation De Beers Group has been operating diamond mines, conducting diamond exploration, and marketing diamond rings since 1888. For over 100 years, they had a near monopoly on the worldwide distribution and supply of diamonds. Throughout the 1900s, De Beers aggressively convinced independent diamond producers to join their single-channel monopoly. Any independent producer that resisted was subject to De Beers flooding the market with near identical diamonds, or alternatively having their diamonds purchased and stockpiled by De Beers to control prices by limiting supply. Luckily for consumers, De Beers' own internal documents from 2014 show that their market share has dropped from a high of nearly 90% in the 1990s to only 33% in 2013.[33] This has mostly been caused by competition from Canadian and Australian producers that refused to join the De Beers distribution channel but also for De Beers' participation in harvesting of diamonds and involvement in African war zones (blood diamonds). Unfortunately, De Beers has heavily influenced how Americans think of diamonds and their value with clever marketing tactics for generations. For example, in the 1990s, one of their ads triumphantly declared, "How else could two months' salary last forever?" Although diamonds are not nearly as rare as many people believe, sly marketing has elevated the diamond to an almost mythical gemstone compared to its lowly rivals, like the ruby and emerald. So how did they become the symbol of wealth, status, love, and commitment? The answer lies in the initial marketing meeting between Harry Oppenheimer (son of the founder of De Beers) and N.W. Ayer & Son, a prominent U.S. advertising agency. Following their first meeting in 1938, N.W. Ayer found that one of the easiest ways to influence potential customers was to create emotional and romantic feelings tied to diamonds. This brilliant marketing strategy and the subsequent 80 years of advertising reinforced the notion that diamonds would be forever associated with love, power, and luxury. But just like other prominent financial vampires, diamond rings have an elevated price tag for that "luxury" status which does not hold its value when the item is placed for resale. Diamond ring resellers have huge profit margins, in many cases upwards of 300 percent, particularly in affluent areas with high-end jewelry stores. So even though there is a well-defined diamond value market, with criteria for evaluating value based on carat, cut, and clarity, buyers pay an exceptionally inflated price. Most jewelry shops are likely to purchase your ring for only 20–40% of its original value, even if it was never used. The value of a diamond ring, like many other financial vampires, is only what someone is willing to pay for it. Imagine my delight when my wife requested a ruby ring for our engagement!

I often get asked by my clients if they are wasting their money when they purchase collectible items. My answer is always the same. It depends. Some collectibles are financial vampires and others retain or even appreciate over time. The question you need to ask yourself is: Are you making an investment? Or are you accepting that the money you spend on collectable items counts as entertainment costs? Entertainment or "fun money" is part of your budget, and you should not expect any type of investment return. When we discussed building a budget back in "February," we assigned a specific portion towards entertainment, and collectibles that do not retain their value would certainly fall into this category. It is important for consumers to do their research and evaluate if a collectible item has a history of retaining its value. If not, we would place it into the "speculation" category. That is, we have no idea if the item is going to increase or decrease in value. The Beanie Babies craze in the late 1990s is a perfect example of a collectible item whose value was almost entirely based on specu-lation. The shrewd, and often cold, man behind those Beanie Babies was toy inventor Ty Warner. He quickly learned that he could ran-domly retire select Beanie Babies to generate massive interest in his products and subsequently drive future sales. Because consumers now saw these Beanie Babies as investment items and no longer as toys, they were much more willing to lay down serious cash to collect them. If one in ten became "retired" and increased in value by 20x, why not purchase as many as possible? This type of speculative bubble tends to only benefit a select few, while the majority become "bag holders," a term that symbolically refers to an investor that holds a "bag of stock" that has become worthless over time. In the documentary *Bankrupt by Beanies,* filmmaker Chris Robinson explored how his father decided to collect and sell Beanie Babies to pay for his college tuition. For years, the Robinson family was consumed by an intense desire to hunt down and purchase rare Beanie Babies. Robinson's father procured and main-tained massive collections for all five of his sons and still holds on to them today. But unfortunately, the majority of Beanie Babies are worth even less than their original retail price. Chris Robinson estimates that his family lost a total of $100,000 on the collections. In contrast, Ty Warner's net worth is currently in the ballpark of $2.5 billion. Better to be at the top of a speculative bubble, and not a "bag holder."

There are some collectable items that have done well to maintain their value or even appreciate over time. As I mentioned in a previ-ous chapter, LEGO sets have a history of appreciating in value over time. In a research article titled "LEGO - The Toy of Smart Investors," economist Victoria Dobrynskaya analyzed 2,300 LEGO sets sold from 1987 to 2015.[34] She found that certain collections (Harry Potter, some *Star Wars* sets), appreciated nearly 11% per year, beating large-cap stocks and bonds over the same period of time. Most other sets also saw considerable appreciation, suggesting LEGOs as collectibles tend to make good investments. Surprisingly, the only collection that lost value over the study period was *The Simpsons* TV show line! So, it is clear that not all collectible items are financial vampires but being able to identify in advance which collectibles will appreciate in value and which will decline is extraordinarily difficult. In my opinion as a financial planner, it is best to consider your collectible items as "entertainment" expenses and budget accordingly. Many people that would not make a $1,000 bet at a poker table would gladly spend $1,000 on a toy that might be worthless next year. Gambling and speculating are much more similar than people realize.

Hopefully by this point in our story, you have learned that purchasing status or luxury items produces a huge financial drain that ripples through time and inhibits your future prospects for success. From cars to boats to Beanie Babies, we pay a huge opportunity cost to purchase these financial vampires. That money could have instead been used for a college savings plan, IRA, or paying off a mortgage! If you feel your life is incomplete without some of these items, it is best to wait until you are debt-free and have made significant progress towards your retirement savings. What could be scarier on Halloween than a garage full of old cars worth only a fraction of what you paid for them?

Chapter 11

November:
Expect the unexpected

Labor Day 2020 started out normally for Jessica and Matthew Graham of Malden, Washington. It was a windy day, and they knew there were wildfires in their region of Washington but concerns were not too high as they celebrated the holiday. By the end of the day, however, much of the town of Malden was destroyed by fires, and they had lost their most treasured asset, the home they shared with their five children.[35] The fire had destroyed their home, barn, and all their family's possessions besides the clothes on their back. "How does a homebody deal with not having home anymore? That has probably been the hardest thing thus far, just seeing my kid in that much pain and not being able to do anything about it really," said Matthew. Prior to losing their house, the Grahams were social distancing properly and being cautious with how and where they spent their time. However, after the fire, they were forced to secure temporary housing with family, and tragically, all seven of them contracted COVID-19. At first, they thought maybe they were having lung problems from dealing with the smoke from the wildfires, but for the two adults in the family, the symptoms did not clear, and they had a long recovery ahead. They were forced to quarantine for weeks in a cramped hotel, with no home, and even more financial losses from not being able to work. While there is a light at the end of the tunnel for the Grahams, many other families have not been so lucky. The COVID-19 pandemic has (at the time of this writing) killed over 300,000 Americans. Ben and Sally Fontanilla were both nurses working in Los Angeles in October 2020 and looking forward to travel plans for their 20th wedding anniversary.[36] Sally worked in the telemetry unit at St. Mary's Hospital, where her patients often needed 24/7 monitoring. Her job involved critical care and providing crucial medication and care for COVID-19 patients. Somewhere along the way, she became infected as did her husband Ben, but as he recovered, she was transferred to a ventilator and eventually succumbed to the illness at the age of 51. Healthcare workers have been particularly hard hit by illness due to COVID-19, whereas many others in the restaurant, travel, and retail sectors have lost their jobs, with peak unemployment reaching a peak of 14.7% in the United States. It is not an exaggeration to say most Americans have had some type of unexpected financial or personal loss, even as others cope with the unimaginable consequences from the death of a loved one.

A global pandemic and a rogue wildfire are both examples of a "black swan event," an unpredictable event beyond the normal range of expected, which has severe consequences. Black swans are extremely rare and tend to be widespread, which makes them nearly impossible to predict. COVID-19 is pretty much the textbook definition of a rare widespread event with severe consequences. The first *documented* case of COVID-19 goes back to November 17, 2019, in a 55-year-old man from the Hubei province in China, though they are unlikely patient zero, i.e., the first person ever infected when the disease made the jump to humans. November is the month I chose to discuss preparing for the unexpected because COVID-19 really gave everyone a glimpse into a future where things are not predictable. Rolling quarantines and closures have led to many people being furloughed or laid off, and many small businesses and contractors are struggling to find customers. Even worse, thousands of people have lost their primary breadwinner to the disease and now must deal with the reality that making ends meet is going to be more difficult. The best we can do from a personal finance standpoint is to "expect the unexpected," as this month's title attests to. This just means that we need to prepare in advance for things that we can't predict, model, or are unknowable. I know that preparing for something that is unknowable sounds nonsensical, but we need to try to protect your family's livelihood. There will always be limitations. Over the years, I've helped some of my clients with some very poignant questions about potential disasters. At some levels, there is no way to fully prepare for everything, but there are options to deal with the unexpected. All the solutions I outline below are limited by their reliance on the conventional monetary system used by all the world's governments. In other words, if a giant asteroid hits the earth next week and kills 90% of all life on the planet, it really is not going to matter how much is in your 401(k), is it? In the same vein, your U.S. government bonds are not worth anything if the U.S. Government no longer exists. So, we have limitations in our ability to prepare for disaster, but if the world is ending, this book will provide you with some great kindling to start a fire with.

There are many different types of unexpected events in our lives, and they require separate solutions. In the financial planning world, we do something called a "stress test" that looks at a variety of unexpected events and what changes might be made to prepare for them. In *Money Milestones*, I want to address the "big four" events that most people should prepare for first: loss of job or career, medical expenses, stock market crash, and death of a loved one. If you have a plan in place for these four events, then you can start to branch out and build in some preparation for other circumstances that might not be as pressing. For example, switching to full coverage from liability only auto insurance is a way to protect you from a mistake you make while driving a vehicle. Or purchasing rental insurance to protect you from theft or damage to your belongings. There are many ways to mitigate the risk to your belongings, property, and livelihood, but I would suggest focusing on the "big four" first, then expanding into other types of protection.

Losing a job can be psychologically draining and overwhelming in the best of times, but if you get laid off unexpectedly and have not prepared to cover your living expenses, it can turn into a nightmare. One of our primary ways to "expect the unexpected" is to build a solid emergency fund. They offer us a sense of security when our livelihood has been taken away and a foundation to pay our living expenses while we search for new career opportunities.

Emergency funds are a necessary and important component of a good financial plan. They provide financial stability that protects your family from making choices in emergency situations that would otherwise have negative consequences. An emergency fund provides you with the peace of mind to know that should something unexpected happen, such as losing your job, you can worry about how to deal with the emergency itself and not worry about your finances. There has been a large stock market boom since the end of the financial crisis in 2008, and consequently, many people have become complacent regarding emergency funds. Why lock up your cash in a boring low interest savings account when investing in the stock market is much more lucrative? But in a post-COVID-19 world with millions unemployed, small businesses closing left and right, and medical bills mounting for many families, emergency funds have demonstrated how important they are to your family's security.

Your emergency fund should be used only for the events that really upend your entire world. Most commonly, these are living expenses from job loss, unforeseen medical emergency, or funeral expenses. Medical deductibles and unexpected surgeries are often a double whammy because there might also be a drop in wages during the recovery period. So, we are talking about real emergencies here, not "I need to have to the newest iPhone."

- College tuition is not an emergency.
- Wanting to upgrade to a new car is not an emergency. (But needing transportation to keep your job is!)
- Buying a new house is not an emergency.
- Home improvement is not an emergency.
- Vacations are not an emergency.

If you apply the concept too liberally, you'll constantly be depleting your fund, which defeats the purpose of its existence, which is to provide security during life's worst moments.

Emergency funds need to be tailored to your specific situation, and how much you keep in your fund depends on your living expenses. Your living expenses are what you *need* to live each month, not your wants. The idea is that the fund can provide for your basic needs like housing, food, utilities, and transportation. Grande Pumpkin Spice Frappuccino's are not considered a basic need, despite popular belief. Because the purpose of the fund is to pay for all your monthly expenses in the case of an emergency, the amount depends on your required monthly expenses (not your "wants"). Here are some general guidelines:

- One income household = more risk
- Two income household = less risk
- Secure job = less risk

- Unsecure job = more risk

- High career turnover time = more risk

- Poor medical history = more risk

I recommend a three-month emergency fund for dual incomes with secure jobs, and a six-month emergency fund for single-income households, or those with some uncertainty about their prospects at their current position. Some careers have a naturally slow turnaround time for new positions, so it is up to you to really understand your field and its hiring trends as well as your marketability. In the event of a job loss or long medical stay that causes a furlough from work, the security that you can pay your bills for six months will provide some much-needed levity during a stressful period. If your family has two incomes, it is reasonable to drop the number of months' worth of expenses you keep on hand for emergency situations. A six-month emergency fund for family with monthly expenses (mortgage, utilities, food, travel) of $2500 would be $15,000. I normally recommend to budget only for the actual necessities, because if someone in your family has an unexpected job loss or hospital stay, it is probably in your best interest to limit the discretionary spending for a few months to help hasten the recovery. Fully funding an emergency fund is a major money milestone in your financial journey.

The last consideration we need to make for your emergency fund is where to hold the cash. Many people fall into the trap of just dumping it into a checking account, but there are better choices. Allocating money to your emergency fund should be the first step of any savings plan because it is established prior to investing for retirement, college costs, or even paying down your mortgage. It is a form of protection and it needs to be established early in your personal finance journey. I recommend the following savings order for most people, though everyone's situation is different:

1. Establish a three-to-six-month emergency fund in cash.

2. Contribute to your 401(k) or another work-sponsored retirement plan up to the match. (Always take free money!)

3. Fill your IRA.

4. Go back and max your 401(k) contribution.

5. Max your Health Savings Accounts (HSAs), Flexible Spending Accounts (FSAs), or College Savings plans, if applicable.

6. Invest in taxable brokerage accounts.

In "August," we talked about the concept of liquidity, and how illiquid assets can be difficult to access without penalties or incurring taxes. Emergency funds should be liquid, meaning you can access the cash easily and without a long waiting time. Emergency funds should not be held in any type of tax-advantaged retirement account like an IRA or any illiquid asset like a certificate of deposit (CD) or an individual bond. Ideally, the funds should be accessible before you must pay credit card interest on money you have spent during the emergency period. Unfortunately, there are very few good options to safely park your cash and earn a good return because interest rates will be at historical lows for many years to come. Remember that inflation causes the value of goods in America to increase by about 2% per year, so you will potentially lose money on your emergency fund due to inflation. Here are some guidelines to try and minimize that as much as possible:

Good choices: high-yield savings accounts and money market funds.

Acceptable choices: checking accounts (though you will lose full inflation value each year on this cash) and low volatility bond funds.

Poor choices: CDs, individual bonds, volatile stock, or equity funds.

It is possible to keep your emergency fund in a taxable stock account without too much trouble, as it usually only takes a few days to sell the assets and transfer the money back to a checking account. However, this is suboptimal, as you might be forced to sell at a loss or create a taxable event. In other words, your stock investments should always be something you are looking to hold for the future, so you can avoid selling them at the worst time to pay for an emergency. Your emergency cash "pre-funds" the unexpected, so you are not forced to sell your investments to your own disadvantage.

Emergency funds help us prepare for the first two events of the "big four": job loss and medical expenses. But an emergency fund is far too little money to help prepare for what is often the worst possible moment in someone's life: the death of a spouse or other family member. To prepare for the unthinkable, we need a tool to mitigate our risk, and that means insurance. More specifically, life insurance. Not everybody needs life insurance, but most will at some point during their lifetime. Purchasing life insurance is a money milestone that comes and goes during your life and is critical at certain times and a potential waste of money during others. I've worked with many widows throughout my career, and the security provided by a life insurance policy can really help bring some calm and security to an otherwise tragic period for the family. Financial stress during grieving is something that nobody should have to deal with.

Would your death cause your family or your dependents financial stress? That is the only question that needs to be asked when considering a life insurance policy. If you are 65 years old, with 1.5 million safely tucked away for retirement, and your kids have graduated from college and have their own careers, you don't need life insurance! Similarly, a 20-year-old single college student likely does not need life insurance. Life insurance is meant to provide for your family and replace the income that you would have been providing them if you were alive. Life insurance is most useful for people with young children at home and/or a spouse or other family member dependent on their income. That *tends* to be people in the 25–50 years old bracket, but it does not have to be, and it really depends on your personal situation. If you are financially well off and near retirement, your family is going to inherit all your assets anyway, so you are likely just wasting money each month on an insurance policy. Further, life insurance policies are much cheaper if you are younger and statistically less likely to die unexpectedly. Life insurance offers peace of mind and helps to ensure that your debts and loved ones will be financially taken care of in the event of your death. But before considering your purchase, you need to decide on how much you need. Calculating your life insurance needs is often an elaborate process, with the insurance industry using a series of complex formulas called the "human life approach" and "needs approach." Some of these approaches are complicated, and not surprisingly tend to overvalue how much you really need. I prefer a simpler approach, based on a few criteria: your income and living expenses, debt and remaining mortgage, funeral expenses, and future college savings. So, let's consider an example:

Madison and Justin are both 30 years old and married with two young kids, ages seven and three. Madison is employed at a local accounting office and makes $40,000/year, and Justin is a contractor that makes about $50,000/year. They owe $140,000 on their mortgage, have $3,000/month in living expenses, and have plans to send both of their children to four-year public universities when they are older. How much life insurance should Justin carry to help protect his family if he were to die unexpectedly?

To estimate your life insurance needs (LIN), simply use the following formula:

LIN = funeral expenses + remaining debt and mortgage + cost to fund education + living expenses until both children are 18 or ten years, whichever is more.

Applying the LIN formula to Justin, we get ($10,000) + ($140,000) + ($152,000) + ($540,000; $3000/per month for 15 years) = $842,000 in life insurance needs. You may have noticed that I recommend paying for all living expenses, even though Madison is paying for a large portion of their expenses. Losing a spouse at a young age can be a devastating event, and many people will want to take time off work to recover and might need to spend more time at home caring for their family. By covering all living expenses for at least ten years (or until your children are 18), there will be a long-term security for the family and less added pressure to go back to work immediately.

Back in chapter four, you might recall that I spoke very critically of insurance agents and their tendency to trick consumers by calling themselves "financial advisors." This remains true, and there are very few reasons to combine your investments with your life insurance policies via products called universal or whole life. They are expensive, predatory, and include loopholes and other "sleight of hand" by the insurance company at your expense. Complex insurance products like this are "sold" not "bought." In other words, they are sales products with a big commission for an insurance agent but are generally not something that savvy investors seek out to buy themselves. On the other hand, term life insurance, which just includes a monthly fee to cover yourself tends to be a good choice, especially if you can lock in a long-term plan (say ten or 20 years) at a fixed rate. In our example above, Justin would be best served with a ten-year, term life policy for around $840,000. That way he can re-evaluate their needs when their children are teenagers and adjust accordingly.

NY Times author James Stewart told the harrowing story of his emotional journey during the rapid stock market crash in February and March of 2020.[37] All his life, he was a disciplined investor, following rigid rules to not time the market, stay invested, and keep to his plan (all things I support). But the rapid coronavirus-fueled 35% drop in the S&P 500 broke his resolve and made him violate one of his rules that he had held since 1987, when a 23% drop in the Dow Jones index made him panic. The "coronavirus crash" as it's now called, was one of the steepest drops in history, even worse than during the Great Depression. In February, the market seemed to be in a "normal" state of gradual decline, after a large run-up in January. But on Thursday, March 12, after President Trump banned most air travel between the United States and Europe, and after several world economies began to shut down, the S&P dropped 10%, leaving investors in a state of panic. Were you invested at the time? Did you give in to the panic? The ebbs and flows of the stock market can often lead to what feels like an endless cycle of euphoria and panic, with many investors in a constant state of paranoia, waiting for the next opportunity. The reality is that trying to time these major events and swings is a fool's errand. I listed "stock market crash" as one of the big four threats to your portfolio, but the real threat is yourself. Millions of people sold their investments in March of 2020, only to watch the entire market not only recover, but make record gains by December. In fact, in just a couple of months, the stock market had risen to the point of erasing the entire coronavirus crash. Unfortunately, millions of people held cash all summer waiting for the market to drop again because they panic-sold at the worst time. By waiting this long, they "locked in" 30% or more in losses, where if they had done nothing, they would be up over 11% for the year (as of mid-December 2020). So, the last step in preparing for this type of uncertainty is to understand your risk tolerance. Your investments need to be allocated in a way that you withstand these swings and drops without panicking and holding your investments. The people who panicked in March had investments that were too risky for their personal tolerance. This is another reason why I think most people would benefit from using a financial planner because we have seen this panic many times and are able to help our clients "off the ledge" at the worst moment. A small annual fee is nothing compared to preventing huge losses that will hurt your portfolio for the rest of your life. To properly know how much risk you can tolerate, you need to evaluate your portfolio *before* the next market crash. If you are evaluating your risk tolerance during the panic, it's already too late.

There is a great quote from Mike Tyson that perfectly summarizes my thoughts on risk tolerance and the stock market:

"Everyone has a plan until they get punched in the mouth."— *Mike Tyson*

In other words, if your "plan" involves taking too much risk and then panicking when you get punched in the face, that was not much of a plan in the first place. I often see investors who think they can "dodge the punch" and their plan involves being able to guess the moment before the market crash. The reality is that most people can't see the punch coming until it is too late. The market rarely does what people think it should, especially in the post-coronavirus world.

How do you know what your risk tolerance is? This is a difficult question, but it really comes down to a few important factors. Investing time horizon, age, goals, comfort, and current wealth/income are all important considerations for calculating your risk tolerance. Ultimately, your risk tolerance is your ability to withstand losses without selling. Why does it matter so much if you sell? Hundreds of years of data across multiple markets, depressions, recessions, and market bubbles all point to an important truth about investing: people that hold their investments for long periods of time make money. Lots of money. There is no better predictor of success. One of the best predictors of failure is giving into panic and emotional buying and selling. It can be hard for many people to remove the emotional aspect of making investment and trading decisions. Some studies have shown that most people underperform compared to professionals because of their behavioral choices, particularly during stressful market periods. A recent Vanguard study[38] estimated up to a 3% potential difference, based primarily on behavioral mistakes and the type of small adjustments professionals use that the average investor does not. For a 20-year period (1995–2015), the average stock investor earned a return of 5.19% compared to the S&P 500 average of 9.85% per year, primarily driven by emotional decision-making.[39]

Time Horizon: Even younger investors might have money invested that they need within a few years for a house deposit, relocation, or other large expenditure. If you need access to your funds within five years, you should not be taking as much risk as someone that has a 30+ year outlook for using that cash. The stock market averages 7% in growth each year, but there are valleys, dips, and depressions along the way. There might be years where the market is down more than 20%. A longer investment time horizon allows for the averages to balance out.

Age: Younger investors can weather market downturns and "wait out" periods where the market is underperforming. Older investors that are dependent on their investments for income are particularly vulnerable to market downturns. Remember, a 50% drop in your portfolio requires a 100% gain to recover (100 to 50 = -50%, 50 to 100 = +100%).

Goals: Investing is much more complicated than "try and make as much as possible." Gambling is easy. Making consistent returns that help you meet your retirement, home ownership, career, and legacy goals requires a specific process.

Wealth: An investor with an extremely large portfolio is going to be able to weather market downturns much more easily than people that are completely dependent on their savings. Retirees with additional sources of income (e.g., pensions or business income) are also able to take more risk because there is more room to accommodate losses in their overall investment plan.

Comfort: People are different. Some can sleep easily at night with heavy losses, others suffer debilitating anxiety over even small ones. If you are suffering extreme anxiety over your investments, or checking them daily, that is a sign that your allocation is too risky and should be adjusted.

Investing in the stock market without an evaluation of your risk tolerance is like getting punched in the face by Mike Tyson, *then* figuring out what your plan will be (hint: it's too late). Many financial planners will have their clients answer a series of questions about their anxiety and reactions to market volatility, though you can find some of these tools online as well. For some people, there is also a risk that you might be investing too conservatively and hurting your future self by limiting your returns, so you need to work on finding your appropriate balance. Your investments should never keep you up at night, and if your asset allocation is built correctly, you won't panic during market turmoil, like those poor unfortunate souls who sold during the coronavirus crash.

Chapter 12

December:
Setting goals and knowing to how to reach them

Take a moment and think about your daily, weekly, and monthly routines. Do you make a list of groceries that you need to pick up for the week? Or perhaps you have an entire calendar written out for your children's school and sporting events, household chores, or playdates? At work, most of us obsessively track meetings, duties, and other deadlines in our online calendars. We organize our lives into a labyrinth of reminders, alert chirps, and endless e-mails. Why do we do this? Because without this structure, many of us quickly become overwhelmed and are unable to be productive as an employee, spouse, parent, or friend. We need guidance, or our lives start to lack the stability we need for a comfortable and stress-free existence. Sometimes surprises are good, but on an everyday basis, we find comfort in knowing what our obligations are. One of the interesting things I've noticed during my chats with clients is how often folks approach their finances with no clear outline of where they are going. While most people would acknowledge that they probably need a financial plan, I think there is a lot of mystery about what one consists of. My goal this month is to really explain what the components of a good financial plan are. Why

December? The end of the year is when many people begin to plan for the following year, but it is also the end of the tax year, when end-of-year bonuses and other major financial decisions are made across corporate America. But more importantly, it represents a culmination of everything we have discussed in the previous 11 months. December is the perfect time to review your goals for the year (Did you meet them?) and if not, what needs to happen next year to get you back on track. Back in chapter one, I talked about how changing your financial life requires some deep introspection and self-motivation to make changes. But making those changes first requires you to have a plan! If you do not have a clear guide on how to make the changes, you will likely fail, and our goal here is set you up for success. Self-motivation in January means nothing if you do not have a guide to follow for yourself.

The first 11 chapters in *Money Milestones* have been a bit of a ruse on my part. We have spent time talking about people and their experiences, financial calculations and advice, and my own personal anecdotes about personal finance. But what we *really* have been doing this whole time is giving you the tools to build a financial plan for yourself, or at least provide you with the knowledge to collaborate on a plan with a professional. Either way, the person in charge is you. All the good advice in the world can't help somebody that will not listen. So ultimately, you need to know what the major pieces of your financial plan are, and how they are going to help you reach your goals. A financial plan is like a highway. It provides the path that you need to get to your destination. But how do you know what your destination is? Those are your life goals, and they represent where your car is going on the personal finance highway. If you do not have specific destinations in your plan, you are destined to drive around aimlessly with no place to stop and enjoy your progress. As you progress towards your goals, you will pass many of the money milestones we have discussed in this book. They are the place where you can stop, say "I did it," and give yourself the motivation to continue your plan.

Before we explain the pieces of the financial plan puzzle, we need to mention what a financial plan is *not*. A financial plan is not a simple excel template that you plug some numbers into, and it tells you how rich you will be if you invest $10,000 a year for the rest of your life. Across America, name-brand financial companies that you can find on every street corner take a quick couple of numbers from their potential clients and do a simple forecast of their investment return over time. These are not financial plans; they are sales products! Look how rich you will be if you just invest with us. Financial plans are a comprehensive guide for every aspect of your financial life and many of your lifestyle goals and choices. The key to your planning is understanding what you want, and then the plan will provide the most optimal way to reach it. Just like your GPS gives you directions to find your destination when driving on the highway. A good financial plan addresses everything we've discussed over the past 11 chapters, including a clear outline of your retirement, travel, and other life goals, investment strategy and allocation, tax planning and forecasting, budgeting, liquidity and emergency fund, college savings, education and career investment, strategy to pay down your debt, choosing a mortgage loan, savings plans for IRAs, retirement plans and taxable accounts, social security and healthcare strategies, estate planning, and ways to lower your risk through insurance.

The most important component of a financial plan is your goals for the future. The more people involved in the process, the more difficult the decisions become. In other words, goals are easier to define if you are single and only need to consider your own future. But they become much more complicated if you are married, have multiple children, or have others dependent on your income. After starting the financial planning process, married couples sometimes realize their goals were not nearly as in sync as they thought. Working through these conversations really takes effort and can be difficult for many people to articulate. It is easy for some to default to "my goal is to have as much money as possible and do whatever I want whenever I want." This is the easy way out! Setting *realistic* goals with a spouse on an achievable timetable can be a difficult task. The overall purpose of the plan is to tell you if you are on track to reach those goals, and what you need to do to get yourself (or your family) on track to meet them. Sometimes the answers are unpleasant to hear. Not all goals are possible without making major lifestyle changes. Others will only require some minor tweaks. The relative importance of your goals also needs to be well thought out. This is because you might need to compromise between competing visions or sacrifice one goal at the expense of the other. Here are some examples of common goals that most people should consider:

- Retirement age (Do I have enough money to retire at 60? 65? 70?)

- Money longevity (Will I run out of money if I live up to 90?)

- Income target (Will I be making $50,000 a year by 30?)

- House and property purchases (Can I afford a down payment and a monthly mortgage five years from now?)

- Travel plans (Can I budget for an expensive family vacation each year, and if not, how often?)

- Paying for college, weddings, or other purchases (Can I afford a $50,000 wedding, and if so, does it impact my other goals?)

- Leaving behind some type of legacy to your beneficiaries or to charity (If I live to be 80, will I be able to leave my children a sizable inheritance?)

- Opening a business (Can I afford to invest in running my own business?)

- Career changes and relocating (If I change careers, how will the change in salary impact my other goals, like retiring at 62?)

Consider placing your goals into a priority list, especially if there are other people dependent on the choices. Your list should be split into ten-point scale, with 8–10 being needs, 4–7 being wants, and 1–3 wishes. Most of us can't have everything we want, so there need to be some sacrifices and balance in our choices. For example:

Jason and Jessica are 42 years old, with two 14-year-old twin girls about to enter high school. They are saving for retirement but also have a series of other goals that they outlined in the following order:

- *Retirement of Jason by 60, and Jessica by 62 (10, "need").*

- *Nursing home costs for Jessica's mother (9, "need").*

- *Tuition and fees for the twins at a four-year public university (6, "want").*

- *A new car every four years for Jason (5, "want").*

- *Moving out their hometown and relocating to the city and purchasing a much larger home by age of 50 (2, "wish").*

Funding your goals requires that your money be "put to work" and earns interest. The only way to do this is to save. So, the next piece of your financial plan is your *savings rate*, defined as the percent of your overall earnings you save each year. In this context, we really mean the amount you invest each year, because outside of your emergency fund, you do not want to hold more cash than you need to. This would include items like how much to contribute each month to your 401(k) and your IRA, can you afford to invest additional funds into a taxable account, and how much cash should you have on hand for emergencies? Many people seemingly decide to randomly put money into the stock market, but most would benefit from regular contributions based on their goals, budget, and cash flow. Other considerations include: What is your 401(k) match? Do I get a tax deduction for contributing to my IRA each year? As part of your financial plan, you need to have a clear vision of how much you can save each year in your different accounts. If you decide at the end of the month to invest your "leftovers," you will never get ahead. Instead, have your savings pulled directly from your paycheck in your work retirement plan and have your IRA contribution directly deposited at the start of the month into your investment account. My rule of thumb is to save 15% of your pre-tax earnings each year. This includes your employer's contribution, so it might be less than 15% out of your pocket. This number is not chosen arbitrarily. Many people can retire comfortably (at the same standard of living) if they contribute at least this much starting in their mid to late 20s. Obviously, there are limitations based on your current salary. 15% of a minimum wage job is not the same as 15% of a $100,000 per year job. Not everyone will be able to contribute so much at such an early age, so I recommend a "catch-up" of 5% per decade you weren't saving. 20% at mid-30s, 25% at mid-40s, 30% at mid-50s, and so forth. Being financially able to save 15% of your income into a retirement account is a major milestone that most people should try and target as early as possible in their working years.

Another crucial piece of your financial plan is your investment strategy. As we discussed in "November," your investment choices are informed by your risk tolerance. The more stock you own, the more potential gain, but also the more potential loss. For retirement goals, I recommend your stock allocation should be (at minimum) 110 minus your age. So, a 40-year-old should ideally have 70% stock, and 30% in a variety of bonds, cash, money market, and other more stable investments. However, other goals have completely different time horizons and potential for exposure to risk. For example, if you and your spouse are saving for a house down payment three years from now, it would be a very risky choice to put all that money into the stock market. What if there is a large crash or correction right before you were about to purchase your home? Your plans could be completely ruined. In a similar vein, if your IRA portfolio has 90% stock because you plan on retiring in 25 years, that does not mean your 11-year-old child should have 90% stock in their college savings plan! They are only seven years away from needing that money to pay tuition. Your investment strategy has the potential to completely make or break your ability to reach your goals. Even slight changes in your overall allocation can have massive impacts that lead to hundreds of thousands of dollars of losses or gains over your lifetime. Your investment strategy should include a detailed analysis of your risk tolerance (How much loss can you handle?) and your time horizon. The shorter your time horizon, or the more immediate your need for income, the less risk you should take. A retiree that lives on the monthly income produced from their investments (interest, dividends, etc.) will have a different allocation than a younger person that wants to focus on long-term growth in sectors like technology and healthcare. The retiree is likely to hold large stable companies like Johnson and Johnson or Coca-Cola that pay high dividends or real estate investment trusts (REITs) that pass a large portion of their earnings to shareholders as dividends. Retirees are also more likely to have allocations to government and corporate bonds because many will produce monthly interest payments they can use for income. Your asset and sector allocation are also a crucial part of your investment plan. Small companies that invest in innovative technology and growth tend to be riskier. They might hit it big and generate huge gains for your portfolio. But they might go out of business and end up a footnote in corporate history. It is reasonable to take that risk if you are 30 but probably not wise if you are 70.

I often see families struggling with the credit, debt repayment, and budgeting portion of their financial plan. They struggle because most people approach this entire category with dread. In "February," I outlined the 50/25/25 budget plan. It sounds great in concept but implementing and following the plan with the necessary discipline is much easier said than done. Your financial plan should outline your entire budget and how much goes into each category. The higher the interest rate, the more you allocate to that debt. Usually, your highest interest rate category is credit card debt. Credit card debt can quickly get uncontrollable. If you only pay the monthly minimum on your credit card debt, you are playing right into the credit card companies' hands. Your $5,000 spending spree might cost you $10,000 or even $15,000 if you wait long enough to pay it off. So, your budget and debt plan should follow the 50/25/25 plan, but you need to outline the exact amount you pay into the different categories each month and then make it happen. I recommend automating your budget if possible. Others use separate accounts as "buckets" to help keep them on track. Debt repayment and budgeting plans will help your family control their monthly spending, and ultimately conquer high-interest debt in the most efficient way possible. Once you get your high-interest debt under control, you will open additional money to allocate to the savings portion of your plan. If your financial plan is a highway, and your goals are the destination, debt is like a roadblock. You can't reach your retirement goals with credit card, personal loans, and auto debt standing in your way. Debt repayment and budgeting is a short-term component of your overall plan, but proper planning can open free cash that can be used to invest later down the road for greater impact. Not all debt is created equal however, and some types of debt are ok to place lower down on the priority list. Mortgage interest rates are currently hovering around 3% in 2021. Should you prioritize paying your mortgage before investing? This depends on your risk tolerance, but for most people, the benefits of investing outweigh the risks. If your investment portfolio earns 6% annually on average, why would you instead trade that for a 3% return on your mortgage payment? But for people with low-risk tolerance, a guaranteed 3% return might feel better than withstanding the volatility of the stock market. Your mortgage strategy might also depend heavily on your goals. For example, if you want to move and use your old home as a rental, there might be a scenario where you need to pay off your old mortgage before you can qualify for a new one. In this case, the relocation and home purchase goal might override your debt repayment and savings strategy.

All of us are unique people with different interests, goals for our future, and a vision of what our life should look like. As true as this is, most of our lives take a remarkably similar trajectory, at least financially. There are three key phases of someone's life as they plan for retirement. The *accumulation phase* is when you first enter the workforce and start building your wealth. In this phase, there is still a long way to go until retirement, but most people set their goals, develop their career, and save for the future. Hence, you are "accumulating" wealth for the future. Roughly this corresponds to early 20s to mid-50s. Phase two is the *preservation phase* and is a period of about ten years prior to retirement. For most people, this is around 55–65 years in age. Most people in this phase start to focus more on preserving what they have already built and take steps to decrease the risk in their investments and other parts of their life, such as career and home ownership. Because retirement is looming in phase two, it is important to decrease your stock allocation and increase your safer assets, though you still should hold a reasonable amount of stock (110-age, remember?) to combat inflation.

A disaster in the stock market or a brand-new mortgage can really hurt somebody in phase two, as the stakes are higher if they want to meet their retirement goal. Some of these choices will be dependent on other assets and income, social security for example. If your expected social security will cover all your retirement expenses, then more risk in the stock market is reasonable. Phase three is the *income and distribution phase* of your financial life. This is usually around the age of 65, but people who retire early or later will shift the timing of phases two and three up or down accordingly. Phase three takes place after the end of your working career, when you are living off your investments, social security, and any other pensions or assets you have accumulated over your life. Many people in this phase are on a "fixed income," as they take a set amount from their investments each month and receive fixed benefits from social security, Medicare, and other programs. Phase three is retirement, and hopefully your plan was successful enough in phases one and two to provide you with plenty of "play money" to travel, explore hobbies, and enjoy your retirement. But for many, budgeting is just as difficult in phase three as it is in phase one, but there is also a host of other considerations that are unique to this phase of your financial life. These considerations relate to withdrawing money from your investment accounts (distributions), and the tax and estate issues they cause are a major piece of your overall financial plan.

Your financial plan covers all three main phases of your financial life, though most of this book focuses on the first phase. This is because the choices you make early are magnified throughout the rest of your life. Applying these principles in phase three is nice, but it will not have the same amount of impact as it does for someone who is in their 20s. However, the decisions you make early will impact the choices you have when you are older and in phase three. For example, if you scrimped and saved your whole life, aggressively saved, and managed to retire at 50, there is a host of new problems that arise. Most people will not be able to start their withdrawals from a traditional IRA or 401(k) until the age of 59.5 without a 10% penalty. Full social security benefits don't trigger until age 66 or 67 (depending on your birth year), and there are significant lifelong penalties for taking social security at the minimum age of 62. Most financial plans suggest that drawing down your retirement accounts too early (before 67) can lead to an extensive loss of wealth and an increased tax burden. Early withdrawals also lead to an increased chance of running out of money, particularly for folks with a long-life expectancy. That means if you want to retire early, you need to set that plan in motion decades in advance! There might be a multi-year gap that will need to be funded before taking advantage of your retirement income. Taxable accounts are almost always drawn down first, so it makes sense to have a brokerage account that acts as a bridge between early retirement and full retirement age. Additionally, rental or side business income can be a great source of funds to bridge the early retirement gap. Finally, it is important to keep debt and mortgage payments as low as possible if your plan is to retire early with a large "gap" in your income. Your plan should call for paying off your mortgage before the age of 50 if your plan is to retire *at* 50.

The final component of your financial plan is your tax strategy and your plan for drawing down your accounts in phase three (retirement). Throughout your entire plan, there are a series of tax considerations that need to be properly handled or you risk overpaying the IRS for no reason. In retirement, these choices are even more important. When you take distributions from your IRA or retirement plans, you will need to pay tax on them if they are not ROTH accounts. It is best to delay paying taxes as long as possible, and that means withdrawing from your taxable accounts first, tax-deferred accounts next (traditional retirement plans) and tax-free last (ROTH accounts). You might even consider doing what is called a "ROTH conversion" and paying all the taxes at one time so that you will never have to pay taxes on that account when you take money out of it. The best time to do this is when you have a low-income year because you will pay less in taxes when you do the conversion. Eventually, the IRS will receive their tax money because even if you delay as long as possible, your traditional retirement plans will eventually force you to take your money out each year, called required minimum distributions (RMDs). At the time of this writing, RMDs are required once you turn 72. There are a host of other tax implications of your investments that are beyond the scope of *Money Milestones*, but I hope it is abundantly clear that you need to develop a plan to be as tax efficient as possible.

One of the greatest fears most people have when approaching retirement is running out of money. This is a scary proposition, especially if your investments are limited and social security is not enough to make ends meet. The best we can do to gauge your success is to run the numbers and see how long your money will last. For example, if you have a 50/50 stock to bond portfolio, we can look at the historical performance of those choices and then see what happens if you withdraw $1,000 a month for the next 30 years. The key to solving this problem is understanding your life expectancy. Nobody knows when they are going to die, of course, but we can certainly make informed decisions based on family history. If your family is incredibly long lived, and you are healthy at age 70, there is a good chance you will need to budget for another 25 or 30 years! Here are some potential withdrawal strategies that you should consider as part of your overall financial plan:

- *4% fixed withdrawal rule.* This strategy suggests you a withdrawal 4% of your investments each year with slight increases over time to inflation. This strategy is widely used by professionals but will require you to hold some stock, so it can be volatile year-to-year.

- *Fixed dollar withdrawals.* This strategy calls for taking out a fixed amount of money each year, based on your expenses. This is great for people on a fixed income but does not consider the effects of inflation. $20,000 in 2021 is worth far more than $20,000 in 2031.

- *Systematic withdrawals.* With this plan, you only withdraw the earnings from your investments each year, i.e., dividends and interest payments. This plan allows your investments to grow in retirement because your principal remains untouched. This plan is more dependent on market performance, and how much you get paid can vary each year but will likely net you more growth than some other strategies.

- *Bucket strategy.* In the bucket strategy, you have multiple accounts each with different goals. One bucket is stable and acts as a cash fund. Another holds the investments that produce interest and dividends and provide your income each month. A third bucket would invest more aggressively in growth stocks and riskier investments to fuel long-term growth over time. Buckets two and three "replenish" the cash in the first bucket with their earnings, providing a constant money supply.

In "December," we just scratched the surface of everything that goes into a complete financial plan. I hope at minimum, some of these strategies and goals provide you with a clear vision of what applies to your family and what changes you need to make to secure your financial situation. This is hard stuff. It is not easy to have a grueling discussion with your spouse about what is more important, paying for your child's college or funding your own retirement. Or what happens to your budget if you take the leap to start your own business or change your career. It can be sobering to confront your own mortality and think hard about how long you are going to live and how you are going to use your money in your twilight years. But this was an important conclusion to *Money Milestones* because now you have the guidebook to put your plan into motion. Taking control of your personal financial situation is more difficult than most people realize. All around us, people are trying to get us to spend, live in the moment, and make impulsive decisions with our money. Sometimes it feels like you are not living if you are not spending. But what you really need to decide, and what I hope I articulated in this book, is what the heck do I want out of my life? Maybe you want to live in the moment and not plan or save for the future. But if your future involves other goals then you need a plan to reach them. You only get one chance to live the life you want, and for better or worse, money is the key to reaching many of those goals. It is a long journey to make these changes, but you will pass many milestones along the way that will fuel your confidence and push you closer to your goals. You can't do it in a day, a week, or even a month. That is why I chose to split this book into a 12-month journey. You can make many of these changes over 12 months, piece by piece, season by season. As you reach the different money milestones throughout the year, and across your life, you should feel a great sense of pride. There is something poetic and beautiful about putting a plan into motion, hitting the milestones, and positively reflecting on the choices you made. Now you just need to get started.

Endnotes

1 Rotter, J.B. (1966). Generalized Expectancies for Internal versus External Control of Reinforcements. *Psychological Monographs. 80* (whole no. 609).

2 McClelland, D.C. (1961). *The Achieving Society.* Free Press, New York.

3 Duckworth, A. (2016). *Grit: The Power of Passion and Perseverance.* New York, NY, US: Scribner/Simon & Schuster.

4 Tod, David; Hardy, James; Oliver, Emily J. (2011). Effects of Self-Talk: A Systematic Review. *Journal of Sport and Exercise Psychology* 33(5):666–87

5 Andrew T. Jebb, Louis Tay, Ed Diener, Shigehiro Oishi (2018). Happiness, Income Satiation, and Turning Points Around the World. *Nature Human Behaviour 2,* 33–38

6 https://www.forbes.com/sites/learnvest/2015/03/06/6-tax-time-horror-stories-the-price-i-paid-for-my-costly-mistake/#1ff89a1d7793

7 https://theweek.com/articles/542936/taxtime-horror-stories-6-mistakes-avoid

8 https://turbotax.intuit.com/tax-tips/e-file/e-file-income-tax-return-electronic-filing/L9DnoQ39y#:~:text=According%20to%20the%20IRS%2C%2020,returns%20prepared%20electronically%20contain%20errors

9 https://www.pewresearch.org/fact-tank/2019/03/22/public-confidence-in-scientists-has-remained-stable-for-decades/

10 https://www.people-press.org/2019/04/11/public-trust-in-government-1958-2019/

11 Donald G. Bennyhoff, Francis M. Kinniry Jr., and Michael A. DiJoseph (2018). The Evolution of Vanguard Advisor's Alpha®: from Portfolios to People. Valley Forge, PA: The Vanguard Group. https://www.vanguard.com/pdf/ISGQVAA.pdf

12 https://www.cnbc.com/2016/08/29/janitor-secretly-amassed-an-8-million-fortune.html

13 https://www.forbes.com/sites/reneemorad/2018/04/30/the-best-month-and-day-to-sell-a-home/#2797ac62fa38

14 https://themortgagereports.com/44135/whats-the-best-time-of-year-to-sell-a-home

15 https://www.nar.realtor/sites/default/files/documents/2017-profile-of-home-buyers-and-sellers-11-20-2017.pdf

16 https://www.experian.com/blogs/ask-experian/research/consumer-debt-study/

17 Dobrynskaya, Victoria and Kishilova, Julia (2018). LEGO - The Toy of Smart Investors. SSRN, April 2018, published online http://

dx.doi.org/10.2139/ssrn.3291456.

18 https://news.gallup.com/poll/6112/majority-americans-plan-vaca-tion-summer.aspx

19 https://news.gallup.com/poll/128186/gallup-healthways-in-dex-work.aspx

20 https://viewfinder.expedia.com/how-to-use-your-vacation-time/

21 https://www.apa.org/news/press/releases/2018/06/vacation-re-charges-workers

22 https://www.healthnet.com/portal/home/content/iwc/home/arti-cles/health_benefits_of_vacations.action

23 https://www.chime.com/blog/5-real-life-money-horror-stories/

24 https://awealthofcommonsense.com/2014/02/worlds-worst-mar-ket-timer/

25 https://research.collegeboard.org/pdf/trends-college-pricing-2019-full-report.pdf

26 U.S. Bureau of Labor Statistics, Current Population Survey. https://www.census.gov/programs-surveys/cps.html

27 National Postsecondary Student Aid Study (NPSAS). https://nces.ed.gov/surveys/npsas/availabledata.asp

28 U.S. Department of Commerce, Census Bureau, (2018). American Community Survey (ACS) Public Use Microdata Sample (PUMS) data. https://nces.ed.gov/programs/coe/pdf/coe_sbc.pdf

29 Drannan, J. (2016) The Relationship between Physical Exercise and Job Performance: The Mediating Effects of Subjective Health and Good Mood. *The Arabian Journal of Business and Management Review* 6 (6), 269-275.

30 NRF's Annual (2018) Halloween Spending Survey. Prosper Insights & Analytics.

31 Halloween Safety: A National Survey of Parents' Knowledge, Attitudes, and Behaviors. (2011). Safe Kids Worldwide.

32 https://www.consumerreports.org/car-reliability/the-most-and-least-reliable-cars-by-class/

33 De Beers Analyst and Investor Seminar 2014 (PDF). angloamerican.com. Anglo American.

34 Dobrynskaya, Victoria and Kishilova, Julia (2018). LEGO - The Toy of Smart Investors. SSRN, April 2018, published online http://dx.doi.org/10.2139/ssrn.3291456.

35 https://www.q13fox.com/news/washington-family-loses-home-in-wildfire-then-all-test-positive-for-covid-19

36 https://www.latimes.com/california/story/2020-10-15/covid-19-tragic-toll-husband-wife-nurses

37 https://www.nytimes.com/2020/03/27/business/stock-market-pandemic-coronavirus.html

38 Bennyhoff, G. Donald, Francis M. Kinniry Jr., and Michael A. DiJoseph, (2018). The Evolution of Vanguard Advisor's Alpha®: from Portfolios to People. Valley Forge, PA: The Vanguard Group. https://www.vanguard.com/pdf/ISGQVAA.pdf

39 Lovell, David. Quantitative Analysis of Investor Behavior. (2018). QAIB Report.